Advance Praise for *Praying with Jane Eyre*

"*Praying with Jane Eyre* is literary, spiritual, and autobiographical all at once. This is a book committed to the truths of things— from the Holocaust to personal betrayal—no matter how hard those truths may be. . . . We can follow [Vanessa's] example of learning how to read as if our lives depend on it— which I believe they do."

—TERRY TEMPEST WILLIAMS, FROM THE FOREWORD

"In these soaring, openhearted essays, Vanessa Zoltan writes with fierce brilliance about suffering, survival, and the kind of meaning in life that can withstand real scrutiny."

—JOHN GREEN, BESTSELLING AUTHOR OF
THE FAULT IN OUR STARS **AND** *THE ANTHROPOCENE REVIEWED*

"As an atheist, I've hungered for these sermons. As a reader, I've longed for this exegesis. This is a book about much more than how to pray secularly, and much more than how to read reverently. It is a book about how to be. And it is told through the wondrous earthly companionship of not just Jane Eyre, but the miraculous Vanessa Zoltan."

—LAUREN SANDLER, AUTHOR OF
THIS IS ALL I GOT **AND** *RIGHTEOUS*

"How does one create a life of meaning—not merely a sense of purpose, but a ritual and a practice to give that purpose structure and power—when traditional religion feels untenable? Vanessa Zoltan destroys the boundaries between ethics and aesthetics with a radical and beautiful idea, one that will ring true to every passionate reader: that intentional reading can empower and shape our lives. More than a love letter to the power of books, more than a reinterpreting of religious practice, and much more than a reading of *Jane Eyre*, *Praying with Jane Eyre* invites us, in Zoltan's accessible voice, into an intimacy with the most vulnerable parts of ourselves, and shows us how literature can sanctify them."

—DARA HORN, AUTHOR OF *ETERNAL LIFE* AND
PEOPLE LOVE DEAD JEWS

"This book will make you laugh. It will make you cry. But best of all, it'll change the way you read forever."

—CASPER TER KUILE, AUTHOR OF *THE POWER OF RITUAL* AND
COHOST OF *HARRY POTTER AND THE SACRED TEXT*

"*Praying with Jane Eyre* is a readable, huggable guide to better living, and loving, through literature—not to mention the most affectionate portrait of grandparents that I have read in ages. And doses of Jay Gatsby and Harry Potter besides. Who can resist?"

—MARK OPPENHEIMER, HOST OF *UNORTHODOX* PODCAST

Praying *with* Jane Eyre

Praying *with* Jane Eyre

*Reflections on Reading
as a Sacred Practice*

VANESSA ZOLTAN

A TARCHERPERIGEE BOOK

an imprint of Penguin Random House LLC
penguinrandomhouse.com

TarcherPerigee with tp colophon is a registered trademark of
Penguin Random House LLC.

Most TarcherPerigee books are available at special quantity discounts for
bulk purchase for sales promotions, premiums, fund-raising, and educational
needs. Special books or book excerpts also can be created to fit specific needs.
For details, write: SpecialMarkets@penguinrandomhouse.com.

Library of Congress Cataloging-in-Publication Data
Names: Zoltan, Vanessa, author.
Title: Praying with Jane Eyre: reflections on reading as a sacred practice
/ Vanessa Zoltan.
Description: New York : TarcherPerigee, an imprint of Penguin Random
House LLC, 2021. | Includes bibliographical references.
Identifiers: LCCN 2020055732 (print) | LCCN 2020055733 (ebook) |
ISBN 9780593088005 (hardcover) | ISBN 9780593088012 (ebook)
Subjects: LCSH: Zoltan, Vanessa—Books and reading. |
Spiritual biography. | Eyre, Jane (Fictitious character). |
Brontë, Charlotte, 1816-1855—Influence.
Classification: LCC BL73.Z65 A3 2021 (print) |
LCC BL73.Z65 (ebook) | DDC 204/.3—dc23
LC record available at https://lccn.loc.gov/2020055732
LC ebook record available at https://lccn.loc.gov/2020055733

Printed in the United States of America
1   3   5   7   9   10   8   6   4   2

Book design by Lorie Pagnozzi

For Mom, who gave me Jane,

and Stephanie, who gave me Bertha.

And for Dad; I write to make you proud.

Contents

Author's Note

This book is a collection of "sermons," but I am using that term loosely. I use the word *sermon* because secular novels are my scripture and I am sharing the best news I can find from some of my favorite novels. But as an atheist Jew using fiction written after the age of miracles as scripture, the word *essay* is probably also true. Twelve of the sermons are from my favorite novel, *Jane Eyre*.

Because this book is one of sermons, it contains spoilers. All four of the texts I write about (*Jane Eyre*, *Little Women*, *Harry Potter*, and *The Great Gatsby*) have great plot twists, many of which, for the sake of the sermons contained in this book, I reveal. If you have not read these novels before, first of all, I suggest that you do; they are wonderful. However, there have been studies (most notably one out of the University of California, San Diego) indicating that spoilers often improve one's enjoyment of a text. The reason suggested in this study is that readers who already know the plot do not get distracted trying to follow the story or guessing what will happen next. Without these worries, the reader can simply enjoy the book. Regardless of your decision, I want to make sure you know what you are getting into: abandon all hope for unspoiled novels, ye who keep reading here.

I would also like to acknowledge that this book only reflects on the work of white cisgender authors. I chose to do this so that I would not engage in appropriation, but I understand that in making the choice not to appropriate, I risk erasure. If you're interested in reading books that inspire me and my work and are by people of color and/or trans people, I recommend the following books that I love as a place to start:

Roxane Gay uses literature and pop culture to understand her own life and big themes in her paradigm-shifting work *Bad Feminist*. Claudia Rankine uses stories from her own life and of people in the spotlight to investigate questions of identity and how society understands bodies in *Citizen*. Daniel Lavery brilliantly mocks and adores characters across literature in his hilarious book *Texts from Jane Eyre* and explores similar themes in his collection of essays *Something That May Shock and Discredit You*.

Louise Erdrich interlaces family stories in an examination of cultures that are beautiful and complicated in her incredible book *Love Medicine*. Yaa Gyasi explores the theme of intergenerational trauma, central to this book, in her amazing novel

Homegoing. Carmen Maria Machado uses literary theory to understand trauma in her life in her incredible memoir, *In the Dream House*. This is a heavily abbreviated list, but a great jumping-off point if you want to avoid reading another white cis-lady after putting this down. These authors inspired my own understanding of the intersection of literature, identity, family, and culture through their works and I am grateful to them.

And as a final note, the experiences and memories I describe in this book are shared in the best faith, and I know that others experienced those same things and would describe them differently. I know for a fact that my beloved brothers and I process our family differently. I don't pretend to speak for anyone besides myself when talking about being an inheritor of trauma.

Reading with Vanessa Zoltan

I am a fan of Vanessa Zoltan, not necessarily *Jane Eyre*, although I greatly admire the novel and its author, Charlotte Brontë. I just want to be clear that my task in this foreword is not to further illuminate this book about another book but to alert the reader of *Praying with Jane Eyre*: you are now in the hands of an alchemist, which *Britannica* defines as "someone who is capable of transforming matter, specifically one who can convert base metals into gold or find a universal elixir." Vanessa Zoltan can take any paragraph from a book she loves and reveal it as a sacred text; that is her gold, that is her elixir, and that is her spiritual power and magic. No wonder she loves the *Harry Potter* books and has amassed seventy thousand fellow fans on her podcast, *Harry Potter and the Sacred Text*. Reading with Vanessa is a holy act.

This is something I know from personal experience, having followed her on a literary pilgrimage that altered my life.

On June 3, 2018, I and my husband, Brooke, joined Vanessa Zoltan and Professor Stephanie Paulsell (to whom Vanessa dedicates this book, along with her parents) on their first Common Ground sojourn to the Sussex Downs in England. We were on a literary pilgrimage with a dozen other pilgrims to read *To the Lighthouse* by Virginia Woolf. We not only read Virginia Woolf's words; we walked the same fertile landscape where she walked while writing her exquisite novel about art and war and the complications of family.

I met both Vanessa Zoltan and Stephanie Paulsell at the Harvard Divinity School, where I was a writer in residence. As a former English major, I thought I knew how to read texts. As a writer, I thought I knew how to write them. What I learned in the process of reading *To the Lighthouse* in community with these brilliant, soulful people is that I wasn't reading or writing deeply enough.

Each morning at Tilton House, where we stayed, we would gather and read passages out loud together and discuss them through the lenses of the Benedictine practice of Lectio Divina and the medieval practice of keeping a florilegium, which are discussed in this book as tools capable of bringing a fuller rendering of the text in hand and its connection to our own lives. *What is happening in this sentence? What comes before this passage and what comes after? What does it evoke and provoke in your own life?*

Every chapter in *Praying with Jane Eyre* is embodied in this reading practice. It was in this manner and discipline of reading *To the Lighthouse* that I realized very quickly we were on not just a literary pilgrimage but a spiritual one.

Our reading was followed by walking, often ten miles a day from Tilton House to Virginia Woolf's Monk's House to Charleston, Virginia's sister Vanessa Bell's sprawling home and gardens. I filled my journal with notations about the color of the walls of Virginia Woolf's study, which were green. I swooned at Leonard Woolf's butterfly collection hanging in their stairwell. I made drawings of the round dinner table, painted by Vanessa, in their dining room. I imagined, coveted, and longed for the conversations that occurred in each room, each nook, from each chair. And the English gardens of both houses inspired me to return home and create an outer space of dwelling while tending to the inward spaces we inhabited.

The context of Virginia Woolf's familial life came into greater geographic relief, allowing us to better understand her as a woman and a writer and how she could give birth to *To the Lighthouse*. Our own words were emerging from the ground beneath our feet and informed by skylarks and flocks of sheep, by the wind blowing through the waves of long grasses and the rhythm of walking together.

This is the vision Vanessa Zoltan had imagined for us.

After reading about Mrs. Ramsay's death, we walked to the

river Ouse and contemplated the psychological toll the war had taken on Virginia Woolf, so that she filled her coat pockets with stones and walked into the river and to her death.

And when my brother's death by suicide occurred a month later, Vanessa, who was often my spiritual walking companion in the Downs, accompanied me as well over the distances of my deepest sorrow.

Praying with Jane Eyre is a transformative book because Vanessa Zoltan is a transformative human being. She is smart and funny, witty and wise, loving the profound and the profane in equal measure. She sees the depths in the highest quarters of literature and finds dignity in the Romance novel. She loves dogs and children and sees the wonder in the eyes of both. Her chaplaincy is one of breaking rules while healing hearts. But perhaps what I love most about Vanessa is her brilliant mind and her fierce insistence on love: the love of her family, the love she has gathered around her in the name of community, and her love of sacred texts in all their manifestations.

To Vanessa, the sacred is an act. She writes: "Speaking out loud to someone you respect will help you find your own voice. Engaging with others in sacred, committed, rigorous spaces allows you to treat *them* as sacred, which is the point of all this anyway." Spoken like a true theologian. There—the secret is out! Or, to use Vanessa's vernacular, this is my "sparklet": my takeaway from the day, from a passage, and the essence of this foreword. Vanessa Zoltan is one of the most spiritual beings I have encountered because she never stops searching, questioning, feeling, creating, and believing in the power of words to save us. She is a woman of verbs. "Love what you love well," she tells us over and over again.

This is the theme of *Jane Eyre* I hold closest to my own heart: to love and be loved, to find where one belongs so one can truly flourish and become one's highest and deepest self. The character of Jane Eyre speaks the truth. So does Vanessa Zoltan. They are each brave enough to disrupt the status quo they were born into.

I can imagine Jane and Vanessa kneeling together in prayer, even in the red room, the room that both imprisoned and freed Jane. I can imagine their prayers are rooted in their shared desire to change the dominant story that says women are less than men, or that class matters more than character, or that the power of one good story—or of many good stories told well and received even as scripture—can truly change the world.

I love this book for its audacity to call a Romance novel sacred. I love this book for its humor and humility. I love this book for both its reverence and irreverence. *Praying with Jane Eyre* is literary, spiritual, and autobiographical all at once. This is a book committed to the truths of things—from the Holocaust to personal betrayal—no matter how hard those truths may be.

Bertha's rage is *sacred* rage capable of burning down the house of patriarchy. What so often is seen as madness in women is their genius.

I love Vanessa Zoltan for her genius in daring to feel it all and act on behalf of what she loves, which is wide and deep and varied. In Jane Eyre's words: "I remembered that the real world was wide, and that a varied field of hopes and fears, of sensations and excitements, awaited those who had courage to go forth into its expanse to seek real knowledge of life amid its perils."

Reading is Vanessa's prayer.

I pray, dear reader, that by entering this courageous book written about a courageous protagonist, you will become a more courageous reader. I pray you will surrender to the magic that Vanessa Zoltan has to offer as a writer and reader who has been transformed repeatedly by paying attention to what a text is trying to tell us. We can follow her example of learning how to read as if our lives depend on it—which I believe they do.

Whenever I am in the company of this alchemist named Vanessa who turns words on a page into gold by daring to read more deeply, unexpected truths are found.

Sacred texts are revealed.

—Terry Tempest Williams

Introduction: An Atheist Who Likes Prayer

*I cannot see my prospects clearly to-night, sir; and
I hardly know what thoughts I have in my head.
Everything in life seems unreal.*

—Chapter 25, *Jane Eyre*

The summer that I did my chaplaincy internship was a wildly full twelve weeks. I was thirty-two years old and living in the haze of the end of an engagement as I walked the hospital corridors carrying around my Bible and visiting patients. "Hi, I'm Vanessa. I'm from the spiritual care department. How are you today?"

I was practicing my newly chosen trade at Cedars-Sinai Medical Center, a Jewish hospital in Los Angeles, far from the freshman dorm room at Harvard where I had been living for the past two years but mere miles from where I was born and grew up. I was living with my brother David and his fiancée,

Suzanne. I helped them move into their house and crashed the romantic beginning of their life together as I stayed in their guest room before their bed arrived. I worked on the registry for their wedding as my puppy, who was the engagement ring from my ended relationship, was christening the chaos of their new lives by peeing all over the house because she was allergic to California grass.

I ran my fastest 10K that summer and was training for a half marathon, in the best shape of my life. I also passed out cold because I ran myself so ragged. I lived with David and Suzanne during the week but would move to live with my parents in the San Fernando Valley on the weekends. I was so desperate for my weekends to start that I would go into the hospital at six a.m. so I could leave by two p.m. in an Angeleno effort to beat Friday-night traffic. I drove my grandfather's 1996 Volvo and listened to books on CD from a boombox that sat on the passenger seat.

I would come home, either to David and Suzanne's or to my parents', exhausted and worried about how annoying the puppy had been in my absence. I would have spent the day with some-one who got an ALS diagnosis or had attempted suicide during a bipolar episode or was having hip replacement surgery and was sort of glad for the quiet of the hospital room. And I had had class for hours with two priests and two rabbis and no good punchlines.

It was a surreal summer full of new experiences hitting like a tsunami; you saw them coming but that didn't mean you could outrun them. But the thing that never felt weird was that the Bible I carried around with me as I went to visit patient after patient, or that I turned to in the guest room at David and Suzanne's or on my parents' couch to sustain me, was a nineteenth-century gothic Romance novel. The Bible I carried around that busy summer was Charlotte Brontë's *Jane Eyre*.

I love the idea of sacredness. I want to be called to bigger things, outside of myself. I don't want my life to be a matter of distractions from death and then death. I want to surprise myself and to honor the ways in which the world surprises me. I want to connect deeply to others, to the earth, and to myself. I want to help heal that which is broken in us. Which is why I went to divinity school at thirty years old.

But God, God-language, the Bible, the church—none of it is for me. And halfway through divinity school, I realized that my resistance to traditional religion was never going to change. I wanted to learn how to pray, how to reflect and be vulnerable. And I didn't think that the fact that I didn't believe in God or the Bible should hold me back.

I, like many of us, have such complicated feelings about the Bible that it's distracting to even try to pray with it. Too many caveats feel necessary to even begin to try. So I asked my favorite professor, Stephanie Paulsell, if she would spend a semester teaching me how to pray with *Jane Eyre*.

Part of treating *Jane Eyre* as sacred has been an intentional elevation of the novel to more than novel, more than art. I set out to make these characters real for myself. By praying with the text and contemplating it as if it were more than a novel, I have conjured these characters into specters, half-human, half-fiction. I am able to contemplate their suffering as if they were art but with the tangibility of their summoned realness.

Throughout the semester, we homed in on what I was searching for, a way to treat things as sacred, things that were not usually considered to be divinely inspired. The plan was that each week I would pull out passages from the novel and reflect on them as prayers, preparing papers that explored the prayers in depth. Then, together, we would pray using the passages.

This proved more challenging than I'd expected. I so resisted praying. In Judaism, prayers are prewritten and always in Hebrew. It felt like too much of a betrayal to my Judaism and to my family to pray in English. I just couldn't do it. Stephanie would invite me, gently, to pray every once in a while. But I always resisted, so instead she would hand me books. She gave me Guigo II, a Carthusian monk who developed a four-step reading practice to bring his fellow monks closer to God. She gave me James Wood, a fellow atheist who wrote *How Fiction*

Works. She gave me Simone Weil, a Jewish woman who escaped to America from Vichy, France, only to go back to Europe and die of starvation because she would not eat more than the prisoners of Auschwitz ate, unable to handle the privilege of escaping.

In the early weeks of our conversations I kept asking Stephanie to define *prayer* and *sacredness.* She, the academic and minister that she is, would tell me what different thinkers and theologians have said on the topic and then would ask me what I thought. Eventually, we decided that sacredness is an act, not a thing. If I can decide that *Jane Eyre* is sacred, that means it is the actions I take that will make it so. The decision to treat *Jane* as sacred is an important first step, surely, but that is all the decision was—one step. The ritual, the engagement with the thing, is what makes the thing sacred. Objects are sacred only because they are loved. The text did not determine the sacredness; the actions and actors did, the questions you asked of the text and the way you returned to it.

This premise is obviously quite different from traditional ideas of engaging with sacred texts. What makes the Bible sacred is a complex ecosystem of church legitimacy, power, canonization, time, ritual,

> Sacredness is an act, not a thing.

and other contributing factors. When the sacredness of the Bible or the Koran is questioned, great bodies of people and institutions will rush to defend them. Regardless of how these sacred texts are treated by an individual, they are widely considered to be sacred texts. In how I was treating *Jane Eyre*, I was saying the opposite: if one treats *Jane Eyre* as a doorstop, it is a doorstop. If one treats it as sacred, then it can be sacred.

Over the months we worked together, Stephanie and I discerned that you need three things to treat a text as sacred: faith, rigor, and community.

Faith is what Simone Weil called "the indispensable condition." And what I came to mean by faith was that you had to believe that the more time you spent with the text, the more gifts it would give you. Even on days when it felt as if you were taking huge steps backward with the text, because you realized it was racist and patriarchal in ways you hadn't noticed when you were fifteen or twenty or twenty-five, you were still spending sacred time with the book. I solemnly promised that when I did not know what a passage was doing, or what Brontë was doing with her word choice, rather than write it off as antiquated, anachronistic, or imperfect, I would have faith that the fault was in my reading, not in the text. As a professor of mine, Charles Hallisey, would say, you have to learn from the text, not about it. I would have faith that the text had something essential to reveal, and I just had to keep reading and working in order for it to work on me. I did not research anything about *Jane Eyre* that I did not already know. I did not read Charlotte Brontë's other works to get a fuller picture

> You have to learn from the text, not about it.

of her as an author, nor did I do much biographical research. What I did know about her I brought with me in my reading. I knew that Charlotte's father was a man of the church, which informed my reading of St. John. I knew that she had experienced a tremendous amount of loss in her life, which added to my compassion in reading about young orphaned Jane.

In Friday night services, rabbis do not talk about what year the book of Genesis was most likely written and how the version we have today was canonized. A good rabbi instead considers the metaphor of God separating light from dark. That was how I set about considering *Jane Eyre*.

Although this may sound like a naive, blind faith, I saw it as the only way to truly transform myself. I was not afraid of becoming an unthinking true believer of any sort; I am well practiced in cynicism and irony. I did not pick L. Ron Hubbard or the New Testament or the Koran for the same reasons I didn't pick the Torah: too tainted, too loaded for me. The history of

Jane Eyre for me is as a novel, as my mother's favorite book, as my favorite book, as a basis for feminist critique. I chose my text with discernment. However, I grant that there is still something dangerous in what I did. There was a willingness to forgo critical reading that could have led me to places in which I would have ended up finding little pride.

As someone who has faith in very little (my family's unconditional love for me and for one another may be the only thing), practicing this form of faith in something was both uncomfortable and liberating. It was not a blind faith, as I had already read *Jane Eyre* at least three times. But I attempted, in this reading of the novel, to lower any critical instincts to as close to a snuffed flame as I could.

Faith does not mean that I think the text is perfect. Perfect and sacred are not the same thing. No flower is perfect. My parents, who are sacred to me, are not perfect. Things that are not perfect can give you blessings not only in spite of their imperfections but because of them. When I was fifteen, I saw Rochester keeping Bertha at home and out of an asylum as an act of mercy. At thirty, his locking her up in an attic and all but forgetting her was not nearly enough to impress me and became something I had to forgive, rather than a virtue of his. Both times, Rochester's and the novel's presentation of that act were generative to me. The text was in conversation with my evolving sense of what mercy really is. The text's imperfections accompany me in my own imperfections and will continue to act as reflection points for me whenever I return to it.

Having faith in the text, of course, also means having faith in my own ability as a reader to figure out what essential thing is being said to me. Even while reciting to myself during tough passages, "The fault is with me," there was a B side to that mantra that was implied, saying, "But I can get closer to something wonderful if I keep working." Practicing having faith in something else means practicing having faith in myself.

Rigor means that you keep at it even when your heart isn't in it. You have to do the work whether or not you are in the mood. You have to be slow and deliberate even if you aren't called to be so that day. It was a commitment, not a hobby. The best secular example of rigor I can think of is the way my brothers look at a baseball scoreboard. We see the same numbers. But they keep looking and looking at them until it becomes clear to them what pitch the pitcher is going to throw next, and they are usually right.

Another example of this kind of rigor is the way you might read into a text message from someone you have gone on a date with. You read it and reread it until you think the "truest" meaning of the message has revealed itself to you. You show it to friends to get their opinions. I was going to do that with *Jane*

Eyre. I wasn't just going to read it. I was going to read and read and read it until things that felt true emerged from it. I was going to do a close reading to look for good news, just as a Christian reads her weekly liturgical passage. And, of course, faith is the necessary predisposition for an unscholarly exegetical rigor. My brothers have faith that baseball is a perfect game and that there is a correct pitch to be thrown in a given situation. The person receiving a text has faith that there is a real meaning behind that text, and if they can figure it out, then they will be able to better manage their own emotions and expectations. And I have faith that *Jane Eyre* always has some sort of important news to give me.

Rigor also means using ancient sacred reading practices like Lectio Divina and PaRDeS, which I've included in the tool kit on sacred readings at the end of the book. It means commitments like: I will read Proust (if Proust is your sacred text) every day for ten minutes (as the author Mary Gordon does) or wake up an hour early to write (if writing is your sacred practice). It means running in the cold and when you have a cold. It means waking up because of your kids' nightmares even though your nightmare is another night of no sleep.

Community, the final component for treating a text as sacred, is the simplest of the ideas. It means that you need a gym buddy, someone to force you to work out even when it feels like the one thing you don't want to do. You need someone to question your opinion when you are most sure you are right. You need someone who points out when you are being shallow or lazy. You need someone to make sure you show up even when all you want to do is stay home.

And even more than that, a kind of magic happens when you work in community. Other people's points of view will blow your mind and open you up to things that you never would have seen in the text on your own. Speaking out loud to someone you respect will help you find your own voice. Engaging with others in sacred, committed, rigorous spaces allows you to treat *them* as sacred, which is the point of all this anyway.

We learned other things as well, outside the faith, rigor, and ritual paradigm. That you can take just about any piece of text you love and apply it to your life in that exact moment. That for something to be sacred it has to be complicated—really complicated. Three people should be able to look at one piece of sacred text and come up with six different answers. As long as the text is generative, it can be treated as sacred; as long as the text produces ideas, writings, and thoughts rather than stopping them, it can work as a sacred text. But it has to be those things or it cannot be treated as sacred. Something profane is only what it is.

We learned that knowing less about the author can be

helpful—because while the author matters, they are not central to the work of sacredness. Thinking about authors is scholarly work, or the work of "fans." I love scholars and I love fans and I am a fan. As a fan I am betrayed by J. K. Rowling and will not financially support her work. But as a person who treats the Harry Potter series as sacred, I learn from Hermione. In fact, Hermione's lessons help me better protest Rowling. I am a fan of Katharine Hepburn movies. And to some extent, being a fan is about loving something and simultaneously wanting to break its spell. I have read Hepburn's autobiography and read about her affairs and love wondering at her relationship with Spencer Tracy as I watch *Pat and Mike*. I want to subsume her, wear her clothes, talk like her, stare at her; not learn from her.

Whereas I immerse myself in the sacredness of Louise Erdrich. The first thing I did when I was in Minnesota was go on a pilgrimage to her bookshop. I read everything she writes and listen to her read. But I don't necessarily want to know about her. I want to learn from her work.

Being a fan, being a scholar, and being a devotee are all important relationships to have with art. Each of them helps us become more human. Being a fan allows us to practice the art of immersion and passion. Being a scholar sharpens the tool of critical thinking. Being someone who treats a text as sacred is asking a work of art to do mysterious things to you; it is the most vulnerable way to interact with a text.

I also learned that there are certain pieces of text that sparkle at you, begging you to notice them and to allow them to mean something to you. I realized that people treat secular things as sacred all the time. Aretha Franklin brought her father's gospel music, its energy and its gut-wrenchingness, to rock and roll. Alain de Botton did this by letting Proust change his life. People I've met do this by reading the Harry Potter series each year on the anniversary of a loved one's death. Parents do this with their children—look at them with awe, wonder, perspective, and fear all at once.

———————

Since that experiment in divinity school in the spring of 2014, I have treated many things other than *Jane Eyre* as sacred. Stephanie told me that because we had determined that community was necessary to treat a text as sacred, I had to go out and find myself a community. So I sent out a newsletter through the humanist congregation I was working at part-time. I said Tuesday nights from seven thirty to nine p.m., I would be sitting in our Sunday school classroom, treating *Jane Eyre* as sacred. Four incredible women came, and we made our way through the book together. Each time we came to one of the passages that I had worked on in my studies, I would say, "This is my favorite passage," until it became a running gag with them laughing at me.

"My best earthly companion" made me swoon even as we discussed that Rochester was grooming her like a predator. The absolute explosion of sexual tension between Jane and Rochester on the night that she saves his life made us laugh. We discussed whether we thought it was true that "Friends always forget those whom fortune forsakes." And we marveled at Jane's famous speech and wondered if we could ever be brave enough to stand up to a man twice our age and infinitely more powerful than us and exclaim, "I have as much soul as you,—and full as much heart!" Some of us cherished Helen Burns more than others. Some of us hated St. John more than others. But we all grew close to this novel together.

I was a shaky facilitator of this group. I was new to the practice of treating a text as sacred and was constantly experiencing impostor syndrome. I wasn't sure if this approach to sacred reading was something that could be replicated with others, but it proved to be a deeply rewarding group practice, thanks to those three basic tenets that Stephanie and I had come up with: faith that *Jane Eyre* had things to teach people, the rigor of meeting every week, and the brilliance of the women—the community—who showed up.

One night, my darling, brave friend Casper came to the *Jane Eyre* class. He came to see what I was up to, to be a supportive friend, and because there is no one in the world with more

positive energy than Casper ter Kuile. The electricity was out that night because of a huge spring storm. But he sat there, having done the reading, and participated lovingly. After the meeting he turned to me, still in our coats in the dark classroom, and gave me notes on things I could do better. They were all wise. He suggested a regular format, maybe incorporating blessings, and other ideas. I took notes. As we were standing up and getting ready to leave he said, "I think you're onto something beautiful. But I think that this would be even better if you did it with a book people actually wanted to read."

I gasped. "Okay. I'll bite. What book do people 'actually want to read'?" I asked, sarcasm in my tone. *"Harry Potter,"* he answered. It admittedly was not an awful idea. We sent the same newsletter over the same mailing list, and on a Wednesday night a few weeks later, the main sanctuary room was standing room only. Eventually, our friend and teacher Matthew Potts said we should start a podcast. Casper and I met Ariana Nedelman, who would become our producer, and we became a community of three. Our podcast, *Harry Potter and the Sacred Text*, is based on the class that Casper and I developed together. We spent months and months planning, chasing academics and religious leaders whom we admired and asking them how they thought we should go about our project.

Over the next few years, thanks to a tremendous amount of

luck, we found an audience and became a community of more than seventy thousand. There are now more than ninety local *Harry Potter and the Sacred Text* groups all over the world, from Latvia to St. Louis, and managing the podcast and its affiliated projects has become my full-time job.

My work with Stephanie and Jane did not stop when Harry came into my life. I had written my thesis at divinity school on reading, writing, and walking as sacred practices. So Stephanie, Elizabeth Slade, Julia Argy, and I started a pilgrimage project, which we called Common Ground. The name of the project was Stephanie's idea; it came from something the writer whose works she treats as sacred, Virginia Woolf, said: "Literature is no one's private ground; literature is common ground. . . . Let us trespass freely and fearlessly and find our own way for ourselves."

On our third pilgrimage, we traveled with fifteen others to the Brontë parsonage in Haworth, England. We had lunch in the café where Charlotte Brontë started writing *Jane* while waiting for her father to recover from eye surgery in Manchester. We went to Mrs. Gaskell's house, where Charlotte would hide behind the curtains when guests were over, as we see Jane do at Thornfield. We went to Thornton and had tea right by the fireplace where Charlotte, Emily, Anne, and that awful Branwell were all born. We walked the moors the Brontë sisters used to walk for hours on end. And we bent over our copies of *Jane Eyre* for hours, in the classroom where Charlotte and Anne used to teach. (Emily Brontë, God bless her, refused to teach. She hated being around people she did not know.) Part of the point of these pilgrimages is to humanize the writers of the books we read. It's hard to romanticize someone when you've seen how small their shoes are and wondered where they peed while on this same hike.

I have also moved on to treating new texts as sacred because Jane isn't always what I want to turn to. When hurricanes came to the United States and Puerto Rico, I was going through an impossibly difficult health problem. *Jane* wasn't up to the task of pulling me from despair. So I turned to Romance novels and then started writing my own. Ariana and I started another project, treating writing Romance novels as a sacred practice. And just as *Jane* got me through a difficult moment, Julia Quinn, Tessa Dare, Alyssa Cole, Lisa Kleypas, Courtney Milan, and Beverly Jenkins got me through confronting the environmental apocalypse as my body betrayed me.

These days, I hear stories similar to my own all the time, of favorite books coming through for people in times of great need. Through our *Harry Potter and the Sacred Text* email account and voice mails that people send in, we hear daily from people saying things like "Thank you for giving words to something I didn't know I was already doing." Many of us practice ancient spiritual reading practices without knowing it. Keeping a florilegium is the monastic practice of compiling a quote book, and reviewing marginalia is reading over your own writing in the margins as if it were part of the text. Both of these ancient, spiritual technologies are things that readers already do plenty, and they do so intuitively, without instruction.

These practices are just the beginning of how you can treat a text as sacred. The invitation of this book is to love what you love unabashedly and to do it with purpose. Love what you love well to learn to love your neighbor well, to learn to love your enemy well. But start with a book you love. Invent your own practices. Many of the listeners to our podcasts have; a stations of the cross for *Harry Potter* is one of my favorite examples. These authors, books, practices . . . they are alive. They are meant to be used by us. They did not expire or freeze in the age of miracles. And maybe if we use them freely, making them up like Rabbi de León, Rabbi Akiva, Guigo II, and Saint Ignatius, we can live in a time of miracles again.

> Love what you love well.

I hope you'll try this for yourself. To that end, there is a spiritual resources tool kit at the end of this book. I can endorse sacred reading only as rewarding, not necessarily as changing me for the better. I suspect that reading *Jane Eyre* as sacred has made me slightly more patient. I also know it has made me confront difficult ideas. And I'd really like to think it has made me practice my imagination and that if Virginia Woolf is right, then that is an act of nonviolence. What I am sure this practice of treating *Jane Eyre* as sacred has given me is sustenance. The moments when I have not known what to do because I am desperate for any number of reasons, *Jane* has held me. And that has meant a lot to me.

Anything Can Be a Prayer

When my mom used to drop me off at a friend's house for a sleepover when I was little, she would kiss the top of my head and say, "Be good," right before we parted. I am sure that for years I just didn't notice this gesture at all. But eventually I did notice it. And wondered about it.

Why did she do it? Or, more to the point, did it work?

I was always good when I went to friends' houses. But I was a well-behaved kid in general. My mom raised us to be well behaved, and this way of raising us was evidenced in even this last instruction before we were out of her care.

Maybe I was good regardless of the fact that she said, "Be

good!" and kissed me right before I was out of her grasp. Maybe I was good despite those last words in her care. Maybe those words were actually a small part of the thousand little reasons that I was a good kid at friends' houses.

It was an instruction, but vague enough to imply that it was simply a signifier for hundreds of other conversations. It was a poorly hidden code: remember everything that "Be good! [Kiss!]" means about using napkins and saying "please" and washing your hands and speaking in a quiet voice and ordering more cheaply than anyone else does if they take you out for dinner. . . . "Be good!"

Maybe it worked magic. Like a fairy with a wand, she'd tap my head, say her spell, "Be good! [Kiss!]," and good I would be! Maybe on a deep, subconscious level it reminded me to be good when I needed reminding. If my hand was veering toward the wrong choice like Moses's chubby baby hand reaching toward gold, the instructions would pop into my head and my hand would go back toward the fire instead: "Be good! [Kiss!]," I would hear and I'd go for the fire instead of the gold without even burning my hand.

But I never consciously thought of her words while I was at a friend's. In fact, what I remember noticing about her words of "Be good! [Kiss!]" were that I wouldn't remember them until I saw her again the next day, after the sleepover. I wouldn't think of my mom at all while we were apart. Then she would show up and the sight of her would make me wonder: Had I been good like she had told me to be? Yes. Okay. Good. Why?

Maybe the answer is that it was all and none of these things. And so when my mom said, "Be good! [Kiss!]," what she was really doing was offering a prayer. Her words were a prayer because she always said them and because she did not need to say them but she said them anyway. "Be good! [Kiss!]" was a hope, an instruction, a last attempt to influence me, a signal to the other mom that my mom was going to do everything she could to make sure this sleepover would be easy for her. (It was the eighties, so it was always another mom.) This was a prayer because, like all prayers, it was an instruction issued into a void and therefore a humble admission of my helplessness in a situation and a last attempt at agency.

We do not pray and do nothing else. We do not pray and expect it to work like magic. We pray like my mom said "Be good"—with a kiss, and with a thousand other gestures. Prayer is part of a vast ecosystem of spiritual tools we use. I avoid praying. It feels performative and cheap to me. Except when it doesn't. When a woman bent in half with pain asks me to pray, it is an invitation. And once, right before I defended my thesis, Casper asked me to recite a prayer from *Jane Eyre* with him, as good luck. He held my hands in a dank hallway in the tower of Andover Hall and had me call up Charlotte Brontë and Jane Eyre and buoy myself. It was awkward but it was beautiful.

Usually I can't pray. But I can read. And reading is my form of prayer.

You can do this with other books, of course. The last three sermons in this book are intended to be an illustration of that. I picked three other books I love and have read multiple times— *Harry Potter and the Deathly Hallows*, *Little Women*, and *The Great Gatsby*—and have written sermons using them as my lectionary to show you that you can do this with anything you love.

Do this at home. Pick up your favorite book, or pick out something else you love, be it knitting or baseball, and let it teach you how to get better at being a loving person in the world. If you want to do it with books, like I did, it's easy. Just read the book over and over. Write down in a journal the sentences that speak to you. Collect them and recite them, pray them, meditate on them, think about them. There are no wrong ways to do this. It's really just earnestly asking a text to change you and letting go of the control as to how it will change you.

Some of you may, in fairness, think I am reading too much into the words we find in *Jane Eyre*. To you I say: Maybe, and join me anyway. Let's read too much because otherwise we risk reading too little. And let's find the strange stuff. The strange stuff is the stuff of life—the beautiful unknown, the exciting unforeseeable. The strange stuff may get you on your knees even when you really don't believe in getting on your knees.

Spiritual Autobiography: Best Earthly Companion

As pretentious and lofty as it might sound, the point of treating any text as sacred is to learn how to treat one another as sacred. Some of the work, of trying and failing and trying again to treat your neighbor or enemy as sacred, has to be an excavation of self. In divinity school, we were assigned to write what they called a "spiritual autobiography." I had never heard the term, and the purpose of the assignment wasn't explicitly named. I found the creating and telling of my spiritual autobiography incredibly useful as a reflection technique. But the real gift of the spiritual autobiography was that listening to my fellow students reading theirs aloud became a revelation.

My classmates became deeper mysteries and were further revealed to me as they unearthed the zigzagging story of their relationship to the sacred. I felt less alone in the company of their stories, though their stories were quite distinct from one another and from mine. Writing a spiritual autobiography is a tool of self-discovery and self-creation; the stories we tell about ourselves shape us. Sharing a spiritual autobiography is an attempt to be seen. The spiritual autobiography, below, is a prayer about in the power of articulation. I hope that in sharing my spiritual autobiography the magic of words works on you, helping you to know yourself better in opposition, agreement, a feeling of sameness or foreignness with me. As you read about my journey here, I hope you can think through your own spiritual journey, as I did in listening to my classmates' stories.

My childhood was filled with Jews. Almost everyone I knew was Jewish. We mostly spent time with family—extended family who all hate each other now and probably hated each other back then too. Immigrant Jews, American Jews, ultra-Orthodox Jews whose visits meant that I had to wear long sleeves even on the hottest of San Fernando Valley days, atheist Jews, a Jew who survived Auschwitz and then converted to Catholicism and sterilized her daughter, Jews who weren't directly impacted by the war but who used the war to argue fervently in defense of a Jewish state. And those are just the Jews I met at my grandparents' kitchen table.

My family would go over to non-Jewish friends' houses for dinner or a party sometimes, but not often. When we did, in the car on the way home, my parents would always play the same game. They'd debate: Would those friends who just fed us, accepted our flowers, laughed with us, and hugged us goodbye hide us from the Nazis, if the Nazis came to the streets of Los Angeles tomorrow, March 3, 1989?

When we were really young, my brothers and I would just sit in the backseat of the car and listen to my parents dissect different data points. Was the fact that our friends had a living room that they never used symbolic of their ability to be organized enough to hide us successfully? Or was it a sign of rule-following that would mean they would turn us in?

It happened to be more art than science. But usually my folks came to the conclusion that the woman would save us if it was up to only her, but the man would turn us in, overriding his wife.

As I got older, I would argue with my parents. I sat in the middle seat in the back, and so would lean forward to be part of the adult conversations, while my brothers mostly stayed quiet, being of much sweeter dispositions than I. I went through a phase in which I insisted that everyone would save us. I defended colleagues of my dad's and soccer team parents of my brothers' friends alike. Of course they would hide us!

Then, as I got older still, I mostly agreed with my parents' assessments. I would offer my own deadpan answers to the question if I happened to disagree. And often I would defend these poor gentiles. "They have two small kids," I would point out. "It would be reckless of them to hide us. I wouldn't hide us if I were them either." I said this truthfully, and yet without true consideration.

My parents, sanely or neurotically, lived in acute fear of their children's survival in middle-class Los Angeles, California, in the 1980s and '90s. And their concerns had nothing to do with the Northridge earthquake, Malibu mudslides, the fire that evacuated me from the third grade that we did not have a carpool plan for, or the brutal beating of Rodney King, his unjust trial, and its aftermath. They found my obsessive concern over California breaking off and floating away age-appropriate and my proposed solution to move across the border to Oregon adorable.

As I attended private schools, lived in gated communities, took karate, got bat mitzvahed, and had swim practice, my parents wanted to make sure we knew that we weren't really safe because we were Jews. Jews have felt safe before. They have even felt safe for more than a hundred years in some times and places. But they were never really safe.

My parents came by this outlook pretty fairly. My father escaped Hungary in 1956 via the Jewish resettlement efforts that wound their way into Austria. My mom was born in a Paris that had been occupied by the Nazis six years prior. And even though my mother was born in France, completely legally, she is not a French citizen. They will not grant her citizenship because she was born there as a Jewish World War II refugee. Her Judaism keeps her from having a home country because she was a Jew exploiting a moment of French weakness. And then there were their parents: I am the grandchild of four Holocaust survivors. Literally, all four of my grandparents spent time in Auschwitz. My mom's parents met in Auschwitz. I met my partner on OKCupid.

So, for my parents, this question of who would hide us was not an academic one. They were trying to teach us. They were modeling for us that picking friends wasn't just about laughing around a table; it was a question of life or death. And it was a question of life or death for both parties.

I was in middle school before I realized that there wasn't a single dinner that would pass without the Holocaust at least being hinted at. Friends from school (both Jewish and non-Jewish) would be over and I'd be mortified; why did we always have to talk about it, I'd whine aloud, in front of said guest, in order to make my lack of complicity overt. The truth was that my parents couldn't help it. The Holocaust, in all its vast complexity, was their home country. Its economy defined them, its laws resettled them, and its language was the base that they were always translating from. So even though I was born nearly forty years after its end, the Holocaust is my nationality.

While I was embarrassed by the dinner conversation around my parents' table, I was proud that my house was a waystation for those in need of a bed. Kids we barely knew, but who were in our classes, would stay with us, sometimes for weeks on end. Only in hindsight did I realize that the dad had just left the mom, so she was trying to get it together. Or my best friend, Kim, who had to share her birthday with her twin brother, would get a special birthday dinner at our house. Or a kid who just got out of the Israeli army needed to practice his English, so he would take my bed for a few months. My parents weren't just showing us how to pick someone to hide us. They were also showing us that you let people into your house, and when you did, you baked them cake. And as much as I loudly complained about being shuffled to the couch or sharing my bed or allowing smoking in the house, I loved the bustle and the excitement of always having guests in the house.

During all this time, I also lived in other families' houses.

My father got diagnosed with a brain tumor when I was seven years old, and that tumor changed the financial and social realities of my life. I never felt like a burden to the other families that would take me in for a day or two when my mom would arrange for us to be away for various reasons. I went away for two weeks at a time with a family to a lake house they had and brought nothing other than cookies with me as a thanks. I just thought this was what people did in peacetime. We shared space. It wasn't a commitment that I had, but a reality that childhood allowed me to believe was universal.

It was of course on a night when someone betrayed my notion of hospitality, with me as the victim, that I began to wonder about myself. I was in Northern California, and assumed I would be able to crash with an old friend. She told me I couldn't, that her apartment didn't have space. I replied, "Oh, no problem. I can sleep on the floor," but she held her ground. It became clear to me that it was because there was a boy she liked who was going to come over.

As I slept in a motel room I couldn't afford that night, I smugly seethed at the idea that I knew I would not do the same thing she had done. But then I also wondered about all the times I probably had done what she had done. She did not think she had committed a crime that night. She does not know that she effectively ended our friendship with her choice. And while if

I was in the same situation as she, I know I would decide differently, that is the point of view of the person left outside. Who was my door closed to that I didn't realize? Who would I hide and who wouldn't I hide? In what circumstances would I do it, and what would make me decide not to? Or what circumstances would I not even notice? If I had kids, would I use them as an excuse not to bring people in? What other excuses would I find? And I certainly wasn't opening my home to strangers. I wasn't sure I could exactly draw out the precise difference between my ex-friend and me, but I knew that I wanted to.

I didn't think that my parents were necessarily trying to teach us to be the kind of people who hide others. But I also knew, with my whole body, that they were the kind of people who would absolutely hide others. They were constantly, to my great frustration and loud complaints, giving away too much money, driving too many people around, and even allowing guests to stay in my bed when I was home from college with walking pneumonia.

They never talked about their radical "give until way past it hurts" charity. They actively hid it from us, afraid that if we followed in their footsteps, we would not be safe. In fact, they would tell us, again and again, not to risk ourselves for anyone except each other, as they secretly sent thousands of dollars that they absolutely could not spare to my old kindergarten teacher, who had been taken advantage of in an internet scam. They were engaged in a massive sleight of hand: do as I say, and don't look over here to see what I do.

Although they did not train us to be ready to protect other people, my parents did train us in other things: Never stand in line. (Your family has done enough of that for generations to come.) If someone asks for something and you can safely give it, do so. Eat before you go to a party. You get to enjoy a new toy by yourself for twenty-four hours but then you have to share with your siblings. Naps and snacks can solve a lot of problems. Godwin's law does not apply to you, for it would negate your entire existence.

There was a profound fatalism in our house that was matched only with tenderness. You never saved the best for last; you used it first. When we begged my father to quit smoking when we were kids, he would say, "I should be so lucky to die from smoking." My father would often quote Hannah Arendt's Eichmann essay to us. But for some reason, whenever he would say the phrase "the *ba-nal-ity* of evil," he would stroke our cheeks, counterprogramming the idea that anyone could act toward us with anything short of love.

That is my inheritance: a family philosophy that suffering is inevitable, death is its only end, pleasure should be taken where

it can, family matters, eat, and when you see something harm-
ful happening, you should speak up but not put yourself in danger. And to this day, I disagree with almost none of what I was
taught.

But as I fell face-forward into adulthood, I was acutely worried that my parents' "do as I say, not as I do" tactics had worked
too well on me. I worried that the one generation of removal
from the Holocaust haunting the dreams of my home and being
dinner conversation made me too soft; that it made me unwill-
ing to give until it hurts, to put myself in just a bit of danger, to
hide someone who came over for a dinner party in my house
and bake them a cake on their birthday. And the fact that I
didn't know if I'd be the kind of person who would save myself
if I had to sacrifice more than a night with a guy I had a crush
on really, really bugged me.

I didn't know how to make myself a better person. When I
tried to go to nursing school, my father said that he didn't move
continents twice so his daughter could deal with other people's
shit. Any move I made toward trying to be the kind of person
my parents were infuriated them. My father, a war hero, was
mad that I "risked my life" playing kids' basketball.

I didn't have anything that I was truly skilled at—that I was
ready to offer the world in moments of crisis. My beloved parents wanted, more than anything, for us all to work in middle

management: cubicles, health care, pensions. I'll never know if that route offended me because I graduated from college in 2004 and the idea of a company that took care of you for life was already more fiction than reality, or if I hated the idea of a "good" job because on some level I knew that the kind of work one does in those settings would train me to be comfortable and therefore scared of anything that risked that comfort. I wanted to be as sure as I could be that if there was a real emergency, a Holocaust-level emergency either on an international or a personal scale, I would be on the right side of history. Because if there is one thing I believe in with my whole heart, it is that moments of crisis are inevitable and I love being at the center of drama.

I didn't have a religion that I could turn to. I am Jewish in a lot of ways that matter to me. I am 100 percent Jewish. I don't put a qualifier on it. I am not a "cultural Jew" or "Jew-ish." I am a Jew. I am Jewish for all sorts of reasons. I am genetically, racially Jewish; if I were to have a baby with another Ashkenazi Jew, we'd have to be tested medically because our baby would be at risk of Tay-Sachs disease. I am Jewish in that "challah with butter and honey is my desert island food" way. But also, I'm Jewish in the "when I hear the Shema, I close my eyes and sing along and my chest feels warm" way. I'm Jewish in the "fasting on Yom Kippur" way, the "three days a week of

Hebrew school for eight years" way, and the "weekly Shabbat dinners for eighteen years" way. I'm Jewish in the "buying my dog ice cream to celebrate Shavuot" way. Jewish in the "Hitler would call me a Jew, so I'm a Jew" way. I'm conservative enough religiously that guitars at Shabbat services annoy me because you're not supposed to play instruments on the Sabbath. And I'm vegetarian in part because I believe it is the modern-day equivalent of keeping kosher. I like to open my door for Elijah every year and make sure to buy good prizes for the kids who find the afikomen. I am super-Jewish.

And I'm not only Jewish, I love Judaism. I love going to temple and studying Torah and looking to Halacha for a guide on what to do in a difficult moment. I love klezmer music and paintings with flying goats. My first brush with the idea of collective bargaining came at the Passover table, when I found the necessary piece of cracker to finish the meal. I held fifty adults hostage as I demanded a bike, not just for me but for each of my brothers as well.

But I am not Jewish in the "believing in God" way. My father once told me that if there was a God, then that God hated us, so he hoped there wasn't one. And I thought, Well, if there is a God, he certainly always allows the wrong people to suffer, so I hope there isn't one too.

So it is with all my love and all my heart that I find myself in temple, unable to get more than a few phrases into the Amidah, the most central of Jewish worship prayers, without being distracted by images of people reciting it to themselves in the camps; or hear the Shema, my favorite prayer, without remembering that women held hands and recited it as gas poured from the showers. I love Judaism, but to some extent I can't really take it that seriously. It's filled with land mines that even if they do not kill me when they explode, their loud booms certainly aren't conducive to prayer.

In an effort to try to become the kind of person my grandparents could have turned to, at least for a moment, back in the 1940s, I was tempted to learn from their stories, to let them guide me in some way. But nothing rises from ash but ash. Their stories resist the making of meaning. And even if I could make meaning of them, I had a nagging suspicion that I shouldn't even begin to try to do so.

There was one thing that I knew I believed in: books. So I became an English teacher and then started to work for an education nonprofit. It wasn't long before I found the work depressing, though. We know what is wrong with our education system and how to fix it. We, as Americans, just don't want to fix it, and that is entirely due to racism and a fundamental belief that if someone is poor, they on some level deserve it. The people who work in education are doing the work of the God whom I don't believe in and are often exceptional but I couldn't stick it out.

So I left education to pursue a master's in nonprofit management at the University of Pennsylvania, hoping to fix a bigger system. My father finally approved of an ambition of mine and I have the merch to prove it. While I met great friends in that program, it was there that I really started to hit my head against the wall about how I could try to be a decent and relatively fulfilled person in this broken world and have health care.

I had been severely depressed throughout college, undiagnosed and unmedicated. So when I was at Penn, medicated correctly and with a few coping mechanisms, it was the first time I felt like I was awake and conscious while sitting in a classroom. I was counting on this one-year program to give me the entirety of the education that I'd slept through as an undergrad—to give me skills to get a good job and somehow get paid to be a good person. Shockingly, the program disappointed me greatly.

Looking back, we were all in that program for the same reason: to address an issue that we wanted to spend our lives on. One young woman in our cohort had lost a sister to cancer; she wanted to work at the Make-A-Wish Foundation. One woman wanted to make experimental theater, so she wanted to know how to fundraise for and maintain a small theater company. And I wanted to make sure I wouldn't be the bad guy in my grandparents' story, or at least not be my friend who found hooking up so important that night. The problem wasn't with what I wanted, it was that I couldn't articulate what it was.

At the end of my time at Penn, I had a very firm theory about nonprofits: that they (with obvious, wonderful exceptions) are a money-laundering scheme for the rich to buy clean consciences, PR photos for their mantels, and tax breaks. Now that we need two-income households, we pay women too little, with the justification of their low wages being "you get to feel good about what you do." White men make a lot of money at nonprofits (the CEO I worked for had a $300,000 annual salary in 2005). But Black women do most of the work, and take home barely enough to keep their kids in daycare. Nonprofits were not designed to disrupt the systems that can turn into repressive regimes. They are part of the system. Education is not meant to educate but to maintain the status quo of white supremacy.

To be clear: I think work in the nonprofit sector and in education in general is vitally important. In being awakened late in life to their rotten cores, I did not come to think of people in those professions and sectors as anything less than heroes. It was just that I was drawn to working in those sectors because I had previously thought of them as addressing the root of issues that were dear to me. I thought if I worked outside capitalism, I would be part of meaningful change, and that I could be part of meaningful change in lieu of figuring out what I actually wanted to do with my life. I still believed (and sometimes believe now) that depression to a large extent meant laziness for me. I was looking for cheap solutions for a meaningful life, yet NGO and education work was resisting my treating it cheaply. If I was going to use my work as a proxy for an identity, I didn't want it to make me a nominally good person; I wanted it to make me a radically good person.

I graduated from Penn in 2009, in the middle of that financial collapse. I didn't have a better sense of who I was except that my infirm tricks of education and nonprofit work were not the catchall spaces that would reward my white-savior complex. I went to work for an amazing organization in Philadelphia that raised money to make grants to grassroots groups in the Philadelphia region working for racial and economic justice. But they kept me employed at thirty hours a week so they wouldn't have to pay for my health insurance (they couldn't afford it). And I had a preexisting condition (depression), so I couldn't get insurance on my own. (This was before the Affordable Care Act.) I stopped taking my meds because I could not afford them, fell into one of the worst depressions of my life, and stopped talking for the better part of a month. I suddenly saw what my dad was onto about middle management and the allures of that cubicle. I called my old boss at the education nonprofit that I was pretty sure did very little to help kids and got a job back in New York.

I had a sort of patron saint at Penn. He was a man I looked up to so much that when he would email me asking for a meeting, I would throw up. I was incapable of writing an email to him without a spelling error. I wrote an email to him once and read and reread it a dozen times. I then slept on it, read it again in the morning, and hit Send. Right after I did, it suddenly occurred to me: I had written *thong* instead of *thing*.

I still adore this man. He is still a hero to me. When I told him that I was going back to the comfortable education-reform nonprofit that would pay me even better now that I had my fancy Penn degree, he asked me the question that had been devastating my internal monologue: "Is that how people do great things, Vanessa? By choosing the safe route?" (It didn't help that in moving back to New York City I was also following my then-boyfriend). But the moment my hero asked me, it became clear to me that my answer was yes. I needed to feel safe for a moment in order to figure out what my great thing was going to be. Going back and working for a sort of meaningless organization that might do more conscience cleaning for the wealthy than actual good in the world was the only way I was going to be safe enough to figure out anything that came next. I needed money, a good partner who I loved and who loved me, and adorable Zoloft if I was ever going to have a chance to do anything remotely in the vicinity of great.

Once I found a psychiatrist I loved, had paid off my credit cards, got my student loan debt on track, and was in a safe apartment with my boyfriend and one of my best friends, I had the luxury of being able to worry about being a good person again. I found myself back at a desk mere feet from where I'd worked before my political consciousness was raised and my serotonin levels were treated. I'd spent ten years working in education, and with my newly awakened sense of moral superiority, I was depressed by it. It seemed to me that on a basic level we know exactly how to fix our education system. Train teachers to be great teachers and pay them and respect them like it is a job that matters. Kids will learn. Fund schools irrespective of the tax income in the immediate neighborhood. It also seemed to me that we, as a country, know this and just don't really want poor Brown or Black children to learn because of a strange belief in a zero-sum game.

I had a lot of conversations and did a lot of angsty googling, because while I needed to be at my desk forty hours a week, I didn't have that much work to do to pull down my good salary. Eventually, I applied to divinity school, not really knowing what it was. I left behind my fiancé, a good job, and that truly rare thing—an adorable, affordable apartment in one of the five boroughs of New York City—to move up to Cambridge, Massachusetts, a month after my thirtieth birthday and attend Harvard Divinity School. And I did this as a devout Jewish atheist.

My desires and justifications for going to divinity school were simultaneously painfully earnest and insanely cynical. I really wanted to be part of making the world better in a more meaningful way than I currently was. And I wanted a flexible career where I could hide when I needed to hide and sleep for days at a time. I wanted to try to be this radically good person, but since industries kept proving to me that nothing was pure, I figured I might as well head toward something that I genuinely liked and tried to stumble my way toward goodness while enjoying myself. I wanted to spend my time happy.

Reading, writing, and chatting are my three favorite things to do. I saw myself as a hospital or prison chaplain. It would make me look like a really good person, but it seemed to me that I'd just be driving around and chatting with people. I thought, hospitals and prisons are where crises happen, so why not go and be a witness? I was less sure of my ability to make a difference and just wanted to get myself into rooms where life was happening and see it.

According to my father, who I love and whose advice and guidance I had always followed until that moment in my life, I was "leaving a stable and decent career." This isn't my amazing memory at work. I have this quote in writing and can show it to you.

When I applied to *Harvard* to study how to be *a good person*, I hid it from my parents like a drug habit. My drug of choice was going after a more and more meaningful life, and I was constantly searching for more and more of it like it was my next fix. My parents were scared of this addiction. Again, they raised us to be as safe as we could be. And leaving a good job to go to divinity school felt like an unnecessary risk to them. They saw this career turn as a failure of theirs. They thought they had spoiled me too much. They did not see that I wanted to go to school to learn to be like them.

I usually tell my parents just about everything. I talk to one or the other of them almost every day. You can judge me for that if you want, but it's a fact. And so if you had asked me, in the many months when I worked on my application, got letters of recommendation, and solicited my transcripts from the three universities I had already attended all over the United States, what my parents thought about my idea of applying to divinity school, I wonder what I would have said. I wonder if in that moment I would have noticed that I had never gotten around to mentioning it to them. I definitely did not intentionally withhold it from them. But I also know, from their shocked and disappointed reactions when I told them that I was going to leave my job and start divinity school, that I hadn't told them I'd applied.

They were appalled. My father, who cannot type in English, dictated a memo to my mother, who typed it up on his letterhead and then attached it in an email to me. In that memo, my father told me that my decision to go to divinity school was "capricious and futile." I do not need to go back and reread the memo to recall that line. I stood on a corner in Brooklyn and got into my only screaming fight ever with my beloved father about those two words. It was also the only time I fought on my phone in public.

"I am trying to understand," my mom wrote to me. "But, I just don't. Please, explain it to me," she pleaded when I told her I was quitting to head up to Cambridge and divinity school. She kept desperately sending me links to PhD programs, asking me if that was what I was going to do. No, Mom. Another master's. A sort of Christian, vague one. I know. Leaving the good boyfriend behind in New York, I know, I know. The good job. Yes. But the program does come with health insurance.

I walked into divinity school, on some level, expecting something magical to happen to me. I wanted to train my heart to be ready to be generous and hospitable at every turn. After the 2009 financial crisis I think that I, like millennials everywhere, was just looking to find faith in something. And I loved divinity school from day one. The reading assignments felt like answers to questions I'd had for decades. I loved my classmates, the conversations in the classrooms and outside of them. I even loved the divinity school cafeteria. But I was exactly halfway through my studies when it occurred to me that I while I was happy, inspired, and interested every day I was there, I did not yet feel changed. And I was worried that I would graduate unchanged and have to look at my parents and, horrors of horrors, tell them that they were right and go back to my desk job.

I also kept having the desire to pray, to feel true humility in front of a benevolent listener. Turning away from Judaism felt like a betrayal and a lie. But so did turning toward it. Whenever I turned to the words of the Torah I would get tripped up again and again on praising God. How could I praise a God who allowed for a world full of so many sins that we now have the Boko Haram? Or a God who allowed for the systems that tortured my grandparents? Or who let us jail so many Black men? I felt caught in a vicious cycle and doomed to live in an in-between space that was one of constant yearning.

I lived in continual conversation with my grandparents when I was at divinity school. Their ghosts prevented me from taking

Buddhism classes (Judaism certainly had enough to teach me) and simultaneously kept me from finding many theologies of suffering satisfactory. Because while all four of my grandparents survived Auschwitz, their God did not. So, like many people who have been disappointed, uninspired, or traumatized by religion or who inherit that trauma, I had to find a way outside of its traditional mode to have my religious experience.

One day, I was sitting in a lecture that Stephanie Paulsell, my mentor and favorite professor, was giving about the Song of Solomon, in a Methodist church up the road from my dorm. And she quoted the line "love is stronger than death." Now, I had mononucleosis at the time, so maybe what happened next was actually some sort of feverish fit. But that line from the Song of Solomon reminded me of the proposal scene in my favorite book, *Jane Eyre*, in which Rochester asks Jane to be his "best earthly companion." I always loved that line. It seems like a really big ask and a humble one at the same time. Love being stronger than death hit my ears the same way. You can love someone who is dead. That felt true and simple enough to me. It didn't say that love could conquer death, or bring someone back from death. But love being stronger than death felt the same to me as being someone's best earthly companion. The two sentiments pleased me in the same way.

Jane Eyre had been my favorite book since before I read it. My childhood was filled with my mother promising to give me her favorite book on my fourteenth birthday, which was when she got it and fell in love with it.

Sitting in that Methodist church, next to two dear friends and with a bad fever, I wondered for the first time if I could sit in temple and read *Jane Eyre* and see if it changed me. I wondered if that book, written a hundred years before the Holocaust, could give me the kind of guidance that I wished I could find in the Torah. I love the Torah. And the Torah and I have brief moments of great love, respect, and understanding. But it always turns sour for me. I wondered if maybe *Jane Eyre* could provide the same sustenance without any of the baggage.

So I asked that favorite professor, Stephanie Paulsell, a favor. In a fit of courage I wrote her a three-line, overly apologetic email asking if she would spend a semester reading *Jane Eyre* as a sacred text with me. She said yes.

Shortly after putting this plan of study in place, I unexpectedly put this sacred reading into practice for myself. Just as I'd been starting to question whether I really wanted the heteronormative ideal married-with-children before age forty after all, my long-protracted engagement abruptly ended. My fiancé broke up with me over the phone, hours after a bomb threat on campus, during which he hadn't returned my texts and calls as

I'd frantically tried to reach him to let him know that I was okay—that I was safe.

That night after the one-two punch of the bomb scare and breakup is a blur. But the thing I remember most about it is that I did not know what to do with my body. I hadn't started learning about how to treat *Jane Eyre* as sacred yet. I didn't have any devotional practices, anything to turn to. I tried watching a favorite TV show, but all of my favorite TV shows are about romance. I had work to do but all of it felt impossible. When my mind is a mess and I cannot hold on to a thought and my body feels like it is incapable of processing the shock and pain of what is happening to me, what is my next move?

I had no idea. I tried to convince the six-month-old puppy that the now-ex had gotten me instead of an engagement ring (per my request) to go on a walk, but she fairly brought up the point that we had basically had an eight-hour walk that day and she was tired. I tried doing some yoga but then remembered that I don't do yoga.

Eventually, as I reached for everything in my sight, I reached for *Jane Eyre*. It wasn't ready for me yet, I knew. But hey—"fake it until you make it" is basically the first real lesson you learn in divinity school.

I found my favorite scene in the novel, in which Rochester is explaining to Jane why he lied to her and is trying to convince her to stay with him even though he is married to another woman. Its desperation always touched my heart, but its catharsis was more on point than usual that night.

Rochester is begging Jane to stay while simultaneously realizing that there is nothing he can do to make her stay. It is a moment of revelatory helplessness, and for half a second I hurt more for Rochester than I did for myself. And shortly after, I fell asleep.

Jane Eyre saved me that night. I hadn't learned how to do it yet, but that was the night I started treating *Jane Eyre* as sacred.

> *Jane Eyre* saved me that night.

After treating *Jane Eyre*, *Harry Potter*, Romance novels, and walking as sacred for years now, I am definitely not where I expected to be when I entered divinity school. I don't feel changed enough to be sure of myself. I have extra linens in my closet for unexpected guests but have yet to take in any strangers. I am not working in hospitals or prisons as I thought I would be. I had the honor of working in both settings but my vague plans of returning keep getting postponed, much like my ex's move to Boston. So I wonder if I am not as called to the difficult work of those settings as my friends Olivia and Abbey are and so am still not nearly as brave as I wish I were.

But I do believe that the practice of treating *Jane Eyre* as sacred has made me more likely to take in a stranger. I have learned, through treating a book as sacred, how to get better at treating my fellow humans as sacred. I pray to Jane that I am never tested; not because I am scared of what I might do or not do, but because I don't want anyone to be desperate enough to need my shelter. But I also pray to Jane, Rochester, and Bertha to give me the strength I need, because I am witnessing and living through catastrophes.

I am less scared of personal catastrophes. That nagging question that dragged me from one thing to the next throughout my career has quieted. And I feel more confidence that when I face another moment of crisis, I have the tools to be a good person in the face of it. I am half an inch more sure that if I face a moment of crisis, I'll not be awful.

We all have moments of treating things as sacred. My family story is unique, but I am not. I am not the only person at sea in terms of how to be a good person in this complicated time, when so many of us are disaffiliated from traditional religious institutions. I am not the only person who feels betrayed or let down by my religion while still longing for some of it. In the time of COVID-19 and storms that seem to rise from the wrath of the earth as punishment for our sins of self-absorption, we all need each other more than ever, even though we are being told to be afraid of each other. Learning to treat each other as sacred is a longing that I know we all have in the face of this contradiction that is our reality.

Don't get me wrong: I don't think *Jane Eyre, Harry Potter,* and *The Duchess Deal* are divinely inspired texts that should become our new religion. I'm not trying to start a cult here. And I do not think that these texts that I happen to love are safe either. *Jane Eyre* is so problematic that whole books could be written to illuminate why (and they have been). J. K. Rowling keeps messing with her own book through tweets that change the plot and keeps messing with our ability to love her books by saying transphobic, hateful things. But I do think that we all need something to fill the voids that find us in the dark of night and to give us things to hold on to in scary times. Because, boy, are the scary times coming. My parents taught me that. I think treating something you love as sacred can be that buoy in the sea.

I still have a hard time finding meaning in things. I knew that I was meant to be an atheist chaplain when my friend Mike called and said, "My mom is dying of cancer. I need someone to just say, 'I'm sorry. That sucks.'" It wasn't easy for me to sit in that silence with him. There are better chaplains than I, who could do that easily. I think that's the job of a chaplain: knowing you don't have the answers, and so being able to just sit with someone in their pain. But being an atheist meant that I didn't have anything to reach for. So even when I was a less practiced chaplain, I knew that sometimes all you can do is be quiet. Mike is Episcopalian, and I know he finds great strength in the lectionary and rituals of his faith. But I am there for the "This sucks, now we can just be quiet" moments—not because you can't find someone else who will sit there quietly with you, but because I literally don't have anything else to say.

My atheism is important to me only in that it makes space for others and for conversations. I wonder if that is the hospitality I am currently able to offer. I love other people's God and Gods. I love Stephanie Paulsell's God and Matt Potts's God. I love Congressman John Lewis's God and Jessica Simpson's God. I love the God that my cousins took comfort in before the gas came out of the faucets. I love a God who calls on us to be better than ourselves.

I often wonder if the God I am rejecting is a straw man of a God; the God that I think believers worship. But then I hear certain rhetoric or certain stories. I know that my generation is called snowflakes and that we trigger other people's anger with our need for trigger warnings. But I think a lot of people are deeply triggered by the word *God* and by traditional religion. Whether they were treated a certain way in India because of their caste, or they were gay in an Orthodox Jewish house, or they were told that their priest would officiate their wedding only if they went off their doctor-prescribed SSRIs, I want to be a chaplain who welcomes them and who they feel safe with and who will never bring up those awful feelings for them, wrapped up in centuries of tradition and power and exploitation. I want them to have someone to call when they are lost and who can show up, like any good chaplain of any religion, and sit with them in their pain.

I also think my atheism is a commitment to my grandparents. They didn't find their way back to God and so I don't want to. Part of me knows that I am intentionally stunting myself. That these do not have to be my final thoughts on God and that maybe God would be good for me. The other part doesn't want to surpass my grandparents and also is too lazy to be devout. I flirt with God, but the place where I feel as though I can be of most service to the world and most honor my elders is outside, rejecting God; demanding more of him before I accept him.

I am committed to resisting finding meaning in life other than the meaning that we create. There is an expression in Hebrew, "Ma ha ya ha ya ha ya." What was, was, was. And that's all. But it only works in the past tense; it is not "What will be, will be, will be." Because we can change that. My father's father was my dad's favorite person. And when Papa David was dying, my dad was right by his side. And my father has told me the story only twice. The last thing my grandfather said to my dad was "Don't hug me so tight. You're hurting me." In my life, these are moments that I hold on to for their brutality.

But in literature I try to drown myself in meaning. Virginia Woolf's sister Vanessa had a dog painted on her bed frame to protect her at night. I bought a print of that dog and put it on the foot of my nephew's bed; protect him like you protected Vanessa Bell, sweet pup. But in life, I try to remember that almost all stories of suffering go untold rather than told. The survivors get to tell the stories. The dead only have ghost stories written by people who are trying to make meaning of their being gone. I believe in interrupted lives, lives that see little to no grace. And I believe in trying to create space for grace to come, wherever I can.

> In literature I try to drown myself in meaning.

CHAPTER ONE

On Staying in Bed

There was no possibility of taking a walk that day. We had
been wandering, indeed, in the leafless shrubbery an hour in
the morning; but since dinner (Mrs Reed, when there was no
company, dined early) the cold winter wind had brought with
it clouds so sombre, and a rain so penetrating, that further
outdoor exercise was now out of the question. I was glad of it.

—Chapter 1, *Jane Eyre*

Starting in the spring of 1958, my grandmother spent eleven months in bed.

Debilitating vertigo kept her there. Doctors could not account for it; they could not find the source of the vertigo, nor did they find sufficient treatment. So she stayed in bed.

Our family has a theory of the vertigo, though, and it is simple: up until 1958, Mama didn't have a minute to stop. She went from a childhood of absolute poverty in Slovakia to hiding, as a maid in Budapest, from the Nazis. Then they found her and sent her to Auschwitz.

I know very little about her time in the camps. I know, because she had fake papers, that she went to Auschwitz a full year and a half before Hungarian Jews. I know she worked for a munitions factory while there. I know she met the man who would become my grandfather, Papa, there. Sorry to tell you that they did not fall in love there (boy, would *that* have been a story). But they interacted several times in the factory and became recognizable acquaintances to each other. In fact, Mama was Papa's supervisor and would "overlook" when Papa intentionally sabotaged an item. This could easily have gotten them both killed.

I also know Mama lost her brother and her parents in the concentration camps. Her sister, to whom she was not close, survived. But Mama, throughout my life, spoke very little about her time in the camps.

After the war, my grandfather made his way back to his family in Paris. They had all survived thanks to fake Catholic passports. My grandmother, with no family to return to, got a job as a housekeeper in Brussels.

Pretty quickly after returning to Paris, Papa started working in the postwar depression that was Europe in 1945. In December of that year, that work brought him to Brussels, and right outside the subway, he ran into an acquaintance from the camp. They got married a month later.

She joined his family's postwar business: smuggling. She once had to go back to Gare de Lyon, sneak onto a train, and cut out diamonds that had been left in the bathroom by my grandfather because an inspector was on the train so Papa was forced to exit without his loot. She alone figured out which car the diamonds were on, sneaked on, and smuggled them off.

She had five pregnancies and three children all between 1946 and 1951, when my mother was born. She moved to France, then to Israel, back to France, and then to America. Los Angeles.

In Los Angeles she found herself working in a factory again. Papa quit smuggling and became a busboy. Then in 1958, Papa got promoted to headwaiter. The restaurant was one of those fancy places where the waiter would coddle an egg at your table to make you fresh Caesar salad dressing right before your eyes. Due to his big promotion, Mama was able to quit her job at the typewriter parts factory. And as soon as she quit that job, she got vertigo. As soon as she was able to stop, her body said, Stay down. Stay down.

For eleven months the vertigo was so bad that someone had to help her get to and from the bathroom. They had to bring food to her bed and help bathe her. My mother remembers spending a lot of time in bed with Mama during that time, and she also remembers that Papa had to learn how to do my mom's hair. He used his acquired skills to do my hair as a child too, knowing from his experience with my mother how to handle my curls. The lessons learned from necessity can sometimes turn up in French braids.

I have no idea what Mama thought about during that year in bed. But my spoiled little mind imagines the worst, the most dramatic version of the possibilities. I imagine she was trying to understand how in one lifetime she could go from being the daughter of an Orthodox tombstone engraver in a shtetl in rural Slovakia to being the mother of three American kids who wanted a Christmas tree in Los Angeles. I imagine she was wondering how her little brother had died, how her parents had died. Did they suffer? Were they scared?

At the end of her life she spoke about her experience in a death march. When she had dementia, she would tell the story on a loop. It was when the Germans knew that the Americans and Russians were coming into the camps to liberate the prisoners, so they tried to just march as many people to death as possible, making them walk around the clock without food or water. Mama and two other women survived by holding one another's arms and walking together. The person in the middle would sleepwalk, the other two helping carry her. Then they would rotate. I wonder if during her year in bed in the 1950s Mama was as obsessed with that memory as she would later be, when she was bound to her bed again by old age.

Regardless of what she thought about, the theory of her year in bed stays the same. I think of it this way: her body had been like a yo-yo that got twisted over the years of use and abuse, and so when she finally stopped and simply held still, she needed to unspin, which is dizzying. She had to stay down so she wouldn't fall.

The opening lines of *Jane Eyre* are about an inability to walk. The weather is too punishing and so the children of the mansion (one of whom is our darling Jane, being the unwanted ward of the house) cannot go on their usual evening march. They had already had to walk around in the leafless shrubbery in the morning. They had already had their time of aimless, forced wandering. But now the weather makes it impossible for them to go out again.

It is not any one thing that keeps Jane and her cousins inside. We hear of the "winter wind," the "rain so penetrating," and the "clouds so sombre." It makes me wonder whether if only two of those three things were true, the children would still be sent out of the house on their evening walk. Of course, those three things are related, contingent upon one another. Just as love begets love, awfulness, of course, begets awfulness. The rain is only penetrating because of the winter wind. It is alchemy that keeps Jane inside.

And Jane reports that she is "glad of it." Glad that she gets to stay inside and not go on her walk. She is not glad that she doesn't have to go out in this bad weather. She is glad that the bad weather means that she does not have to go on a walk at all.

As punishing as I am sure Mama's vertigo was, I wonder if she too was glad of it. I wonder if it was a relief to not be able to get out of bed, to have to stay down. Sometimes there is no better feeling than that of having no choice. And there must have been something a bit delicious, at least sometimes, about having a warm, safe bed to be in after all those years of running, and having no choice but to stay in that warm, safe bed and have her needs tended to. I'm sure it was awful in many ways, like the wind, the rain, and the clouds. But maybe it was also a relief.

When I was sixteen years old, over forty years after Mama's first forced stay in bed, her back broke. She had cement put in between the vertebrae, but she still couldn't hold herself up. So in 1998, she went back to bed and stayed there for the rest of her life.

Right around then, I was in a high school play that did not have rehearsal on Wednesdays, so I would go and nap with her after school on that one day a week. We would hold hands and sleep. I think I just wanted a nap and couldn't justify it unless I was in bed with my Holocaust-surviving grandmother. But I loved the time we spent in bed together. She could be a mean woman for most of my childhood. But when she went back to bed in 1998, she became kind. So I was in bed with a kind, gentle woman who looked and smelled exactly like my grandmother.

I know some of what she thought about then. This was when she talked about the death march on a loop. She talked about what she had eaten that day, and I'm guessing she thought a lot about her needs and her pain and how to ease it. She made a lot of snarky and truly funny jokes at other people's expense. She talked about who had visited her and who had not. She talked about doctor visits. She writhed in pain. She welcomed her visitors. She watched *Jeopardy!* with Papa.

She died in that bed in April 2005.

I have depression that at times feels like a rain so penetrating that I cannot get out of bed. Depression sleep is different from the delicious naps I got used to on those Wednesday afternoons, and it is different from the naps I still take sometimes. I also have endometriosis, which is a physical pain that comes and goes in great extremes. And sometimes I am glad for the flare-up of my physical pain symptoms. It's like my body is giving me proof, an excuse to stay in bed. Look! It's not in my head. It is real! It's not that I don't want to go on a walk. It's pouring rain with punishing wind!

There have been many times in my life I have spent in bed. When I was undiagnosed as a depressive in college, I would often spend weeks at a time in bed, lying to professors and to friends in an endless dance of covering up what I was convinced was laziness. (I am still not completely convinced that it was not.) I had mono at the age of thirty, and if I tried to walk I would faint. And at thirty-three, after a tough breakup, running around, and working eighty-hour weeks for six months, I donated blood and then thirty minutes later fainted onto a patient who had just given birth and whose newborn was ill, with whom I was supposed to be doing a chaplain visit. I woke from my fall and had vertigo. I had it for two weeks and no doctor could account for it. It went away either because I went to an acupuncturist who healed me or because it was two weeks since the vertigo had started and vertigo often goes away after two weeks.

Part of what I think about when I am in bed is obviously a self-indulgent notion of my own weakness. Mama stayed in bed after time in concentration camps, miscarriages, loss of parents and siblings, a death march, and an actual broken back. What is my excuse? I would like to tell myself a story of multigenerational trauma. I would like to tell myself that I am staying in bed to keep Mama's ghost company. When I am in bed now, depressed and sometimes also with back pain so bad that I cannot sit or stand, I can feel Mama's hand in mine like a phantom limb, a judgment, inspiration, excuse, and benediction all in one. But I know that my reasons are not as good as hers were.

I envy that Mama's broken back and vertigo made getting out of bed "out of the question," and I realize that thought is like saying I am jealous of Anne Frank for being stuck in an attic with a boy she had a crush on.

There is a lot at risk for me if I let go of the guilt that I feel when I am in bed. If I do not feel guilty, it means I am ungrateful for the privilege I have that has allowed me softer reasons to spend so much time in bed, compared with Mama. The key is to make sure, like Jane, and like Mama, to walk around when the weather is fine enough, even if it is only in leafless shrubbery. The answer to my guilt is to make the most of what my body and mind are capable of on the days when I am not in bed. That way, on the days when my body and mind betray me, I can be glad of it.

CHAPTER TWO

On Fear

A sense of dreary consecration had guarded
[the red room] from frequent intrusion.

—Chapter 2, *Jane Eyre*

I am not an anxious person by nature. I love being at rest, which is a disposition that resists anxiety. I don't mind heights, flying, spiders, or snakes. But in my commitment to being willing to confront darkness, I have cultivated a relationship with fear. I have judged other people's relationships with Lady Fear. That is how phobias work: they make no sense to people on the outside of them.

Every time I pull a tick off the dog, I make sure to think about climate change. Whenever my dad goes into surgery, I consider that he'll die. Whenever I need an antibiotic, I think about what will happen with increased antibiotic resistance. I will not be the idiot who didn't see the catastrophe coming.

By the time I met my father's mother, whom we called Anyu, she was not a very nice person. When I was little, she would visit us and Mama and Papa for three weeks a year. She'd fly from Holon, Israel, to us in Los Angeles to spend time with her only son, who had settled down halfway around the world from her, and her grandchildren. We never went to visit her— not until I was nineteen years old and could go on my own.

The nicer you were to Anyu, the meaner she would be to you. She loved us and was loving in her own way, but she would seem to erupt in anger as if at a phantom. Whoever was in her path, she'd unleash her anger on them if she felt the need. And she was like a homing missile. She hit you where it hurt, even if you'd done nothing to elicit it. She was the one who taught me that we all walk around with ways that we can easily be hurt.

It's best to not diagnose the dead. But I do believe she had undiagnosed (or diagnosed but not shared with us) bipolar disorder. I also have done some really basic research on epigenetics. I wonder who she would have been if she had not gone through all that she had gone through.

Anyu was a remarkable woman. She was raised as an heiress to a lumber fortune. Even though she was a woman with two brothers, her father trained her in the family business alongside the boys. She married a man she was crazy about, a brilliant young writer without a penny to his name. And then, within a year of their wedding, he got carted off to the labor camps.

She got deported from Hungary to the concentration camps pretty late—May 1944—with the rest of the Hungarian Jews. At that point Jews were coming into Auschwitz so fast that the Nazis didn't tattoo them or maintain their standards of fastidious record keeping. Too many people being brought in to keep track of.

In the chaos of the day of selection, upon arriving at Auschwitz, Anyu was separated from her parents. But she saw her father, who was in a line near hers. He was confused, probably from the days of traveling and starving on the train. He wandered out of line at the sight of her. And she was scared he'd get shot, so she sent him back to his line, hoping to spare his life. She did not know that she was ushering him back to the line to the gas chambers. But I love that instinct in her. It is an instinct I have myself, an instinct to take charge without all the information. Someone needs to lead in the midst of chaos. And she probably wasn't wrong. My great-grandfather probably would have been shot or beaten for stepping out of line. But if anything could flip the switch on a gene to act out her life spewing random punishment to innocent passersby, any number of incidents she survived that are similar to this one (one that I happen to loosely know about) could be the culprit.

I force myself to picture my great-grandparents, cousins,

aunts, and uncles in the gas chambers not infrequently. At the sound of my favorite prayer, the Shema, I make myself feel their voices in my ears, reciting it as they knew what was happening. And sometimes, in that exercise, I can feel a nearly silent echo of the fear I imagine they felt in the moments before the gas was released. I imagine that I can smell a faint perfume of the desperation that screamed inside their chests, not for themselves, but for their loved ones in the same chambers, dying the same deaths. Or the fear my great-grandmother might have felt for the daughter she was leaving behind to work in Auschwitz. Maybe my great-grandmother was grateful for her own quick, painless death in comparison to her daughter's survival.

In 2006, when I was twenty-four years old, my parents, brothers, Papa, and I all flew from the United States to Israel to spend ten days there together. We visited with Anyu while we were there, although that was not the purpose of our trip. She still lived in the one-bedroom apartment that she, my grandfather, and my father had been assigned to in 1956 when they arrived as Hungarian refugees in Israel. She had gone from being one of the wealthiest women in Romania, where she was born, to cooking in a kitchen smaller than the dining room table she grew up with and with her valuables hidden in the ice cream.

The reason that we went to Israel was that my recently deceased grandmother, Mama, was being honored at a Holocaust memorial in Ramat Gan. Mama had made a statue of a man blowing a shofar on top of piled bricks from the crematorium. We were there to lay a wreath in her honor. Anyu, my cousins, and other family friends came to the memorial, of course.

It was there, in the kibbitzing that happened after the service, that I met a friend of Anyu's. I don't remember his name, but they were holding each other's arms and laughing. I went up to them and this man said in my favorite language (English with a thick Hungarian/Hebrew accent), "We are laughing because this is the first time in fifty years that I have seen your grandmother in clothes!" My eyes widened in shock. "I only ever see her in her bathing suit!" They both laughed at me— falling for their sexy trick.

My grandmother was a member of the municipal pool and did thirty laps a day, six days a week until the last year of her life. I guess this man was there doing his laps alongside her. After he was done laughing at me, he continued, "I knew your grandmother in Auschwitz. She was a saint. She would take care of the dying in her barrack. Go and get the soup for them." Anyu let him talk for a minute but didn't look at me. She smiled affectionately at her friend. She smiled affectionately at this version of herself. She had blown up most of the relationships in her life. But this man knew her as a swimmer and a saint.

There is a woman whose letters I love and who was an incredibly complicated person. She was a Dutch Jew named Etty Hillesum, a beautiful writer and thinker. In the introduction to her diaries and letters, her biographer wrote that in the Jewish ghetto of Westerbork "her soul found its deepest expression: she placed herself unreservedly at the service of her people." And Etty did this in large part because she was afraid.

What is always remarkable to me when I think of my ancestors and what they must have been feeling is the way that they must have felt fear. I wonder if it was fear as a kind of despair. There are a few moments in my life when I can remember fear mixed with despair, by which I mean fear and a simultaneous feeling of being unable to change your fate. I remember my mom taking us to the meanest swim teacher around. My mom believed (correctly, in my opinion) that swimming well was a lifesaving skill. But I would be scared and incredulous as she would take us back to Miss Becky, who would throw us in the water and yell and blow her whistle at us at six in the morning. I was scared of Miss Becky, and I could not wrap my head around the reality that I had no control over my situation. No matter how hard I cried or begged or reasoned (at the age of four), my mother was going to keep taking us back to Miss Becky. It was the feeling that I could scream until I ran out of breath and it would not change my fate that gave my fear the desperate edge. I remember feeling the same panic when I had to get my booster shots when I was seven. Not being of a fearful disposition, what scared me was not the thing itself, but the fact that something unpleasant was about to take place and I couldn't stop it. What scared me was my own lack of power.

Almost all of my terror was wrapped up in privilege—access to swim lessons and doctors. But not my grandparents' terror. And not Jane's. Their fears were of clear and present dangers. But I still wonder if what was so maddening about those fears was the lack of control.

I make myself uncomfortable when I try to imagine my grandparents' terror. Who am I to play make-believe with their reality? Isn't what I am doing, by trying to conjure the fear that I imagine they must have felt, a form of self-congratulatory artifice? When an outline of what I suspect their fear might have been overcomes me, I push the tempting ghost away. I want to not look away from their fear but I also never try to understand it, because I know that I never will.

It seems exploitative to even pretend to be able to imagine my grandparents' or other victims' abysses. But to make it entirely other or unthinkable or unfathomable also is a monstrous act. It is important to remember that they were people, just like me. They, in fact, were younger than I am now when they experienced much of their fear and terror. They weren't exceptional. They had crushes and petty thoughts and feelings along with their heroism and their terror. Anyu was mean. She was also a saint and a swimmer. Even victims are complicated. Even the purest victims' pain is complicated. But it is important to feel the ghost fear of others. Trying to feel other people's fear is the most important kind of empathy. If fear is all about a lack of power or control, then in empathizing with one another's fear, we are trying to reconfigure who has that control and whether we can change that equation.

Jane can help me walk the line between these two contradictory necessities, of knowing and not knowing terror that isn't mine, because I can contemplate hers without risking demeaning anyone. Jane has a moment of abject terror in the red room, in chapter two of the novel. The red room is where she gets the sense that there are certain cruelties that the loudest of her screams and strongest of her kicks are not going to change. And for Jane, this sense of the endless ability of the world to frighten us does not come with the added benefit of being able to swim or the safety and protection of vaccinations. This newfound, bone-deep knowledge of horror that she cannot keep at bay comes with no lesson other than itself, which is an essential component of true terror.

The reason the novel opens on the day it does is because of this remarkable incident in Jane's life. In fact, this event, which is described in chapter two, sets all the events thereafter in motion. Jane has just been hit on the head by her cousin John Reed, completely unprompted, in fact while explicitly hiding from him. She is bleeding quite badly from the wound; head wounds are bloody. Being struck on the head with a weapon for absolutely no reason is not the remarkable or fearful thing that happens to Jane. Her cousin John, several years older and twice her size, is often abusive and so she is used to these types of incidents and torments—and while she tries to avoid their unpleasantness and will try to fight back against him once it becomes clear that she cannot avoid it, John Reed's eruptions of violence do not deeply shake her.

What does shake her is the fact that she is punished for fighting back: she is sent into the "red-room," which is the rarely used room where her uncle died. It's a domestic abuse narrative of the 1800s—men hitting women is legal; women hitting back is not. Jane, with the hearty help of what she has just gone through and what she always has to endure by living in this house, works herself up into a state. She is scared that her uncle's ghost haunts the room that she has been locked in. As she convinces herself more and more of this possibility, she begins to scream, tries to escape, and finds the door locked, which terrifies her further. She has reason for feeling this way; she tells us that since the day of her uncle's death, "a sense of dreary consecration had guarded [the red room] from frequent intrusion."

There is a culture in this house of leaving the room alone. So of course she is scared of being locked in it.

At first, she isn't sure that she is locked in; she wonders if the punishment is merely a psychological one in which the test is her obedience. She checks the door and she is in fact also physically trapped. She remembers, "What a consternation of soul was mine that dreary afternoon! How all my brain was in tumult, and all my heart in insurrection!" This is what she is feeling as she sits on her stool for hours. To an outside observer, she would look like a little girl who is taking her punishment. But in reality, she is mounting a mutiny of the soul.

After it begins to get dark in the room, after sitting on her punishment stool for hours, an image of herself captured in the mirror begins to haunt her. She tells us:

> I can now conjecture readily that this streak of light was, in all likelihood, a gleam from a lantern, carried by someone across the lawn: but then, prepared as my mind was for horror, shaken as my nerves were by agitation, I thought the swift-darting beam was a herald of some coming vision from another world.

We often look back on moments of being trapped and suffering and make meaning of them. Jane doesn't. She admits, "I grew by degrees cold as a stone, and then my courage sank." She knows that when our basic needs aren't met, we are more likely to lose power, and fear is what overtakes us. Jane is deeply unsentimental about this horrific moment and I love that about her.

I know that what a lot of people in this fear space do is drop to their knees and pray. Or there are the famous fight, flight, freeze, or fawn options that are outlined for us. These moments are proverbial foxholes, and as the saying goes, you won't find atheists there. I have been trained my whole life to be an atheist everywhere. Especially in a foxhole. That's where the true test of an atheist lies. That's where the "fuck you, God" matters most. On the stools in the red rooms and in the middle of pandemics, those are the times to resist the feelings of meaning. I want to feel the fear, the tyranny of despair, the horror of no one being able to hear me scream. But in the gas chambers, I want a Shema to rise up within us all.

I don't know that I could map the exact distinction between the locations of the red rooms and the gas chambers. They might be very close neighbors. Fear can be a motivator for making excellent choices or really poor ones. My partner is a cyclist; he commutes via bicycle whether there is sun or snow, and every time I hear about a fatal bike accident in the Boston area I make sure that our legal resources are better shored up than they were before (or I at least make a mental note to do so). The fear of losing him motivates me to take action; it reminds me of mortality. I kiss him extra hard on those days. But there are fears that get us to make bad choices too. There was the person I dated for far too long, afraid that I'd never find anyone better. We cannot walk through the world afraid, but also, I could not swim through the world thinking that my mother was going to be able to save me from every uncomfortable moment in water.

Jane doesn't seem to choose fight, flight, freeze, fawn, or pray. Her terror in the red room causes her to lose consciousness. She faints and has to be carried to bed. The terror takes her over. She goes from being internally rebellious, a proper emotional pirate, to simply being a lifeless victim. The line between the two is nothing more than a mere moment.

The Reeds are not intentionally engaging in torture any more than my mother was. But they are not only immune to Jane's terror, they are annoyed with her for it, while my mother sat at the pool's edge and cried in solidarity.

Mrs. Reed is so deaf to Jane's screams that the only thing that stops Jane's screaming is her fainting. And I wonder if what terrorizes Jane is the realization that Aunt Reed would let her stay in there no matter if the ghost was real or not. I think back on that time with Miss Becky as a moment of realization that my mother wouldn't be able to save me from everything. But really, if she saw anything that she pedagogically disagreed with, I'd have been snapped up and taken home, taught to swim elsewhere. Unconditional love with a pinch of privilege is sometimes all you need to keep you on the stool of fear, rather than trying to knock down the door or falling to the floor unconscious.

What Jane truly confronts in that room is how alone she is. She confronts the fact that Aunt Reed is capable of shutting her out. Jane remarks to herself in that room that she always knew if her uncle—the very one who died in this room—had lived, he would have been kind to her. That grotesque joke of what could have been makes the harshness of the locked door all the harder to endure.

This moment in the red room ends up freeing Jane. A doctor gets called because her fainting becomes a prolonged, undefined fit, and it is that doctor whom she finally tells how abused she is and who recommends she go away to boarding school. I think moments of fear, as long as they are not prolonged, can be incredibly helpful. Fear makes us reach out our hands. Fear makes us look for other eyes to make contact with. Fears make us sing out prayers.

It is important to feel entirely alone in order to appreciate or find your community. It is important to entertain the worst possible version of reality so we are ready with our earthquake packs of extra flashlights and batteries. But we mostly only hear of those who were afraid but survived and thrived. The people who beat their fear tell the stories. Jane does not beat her fear. She is rescued poorly from it. She only happens to live to tell the tale. She is a Virgil of fear, one who can tell me a version of the story that my family didn't survive. Jane fainted and got to be resuscitated; many don't. Forcing myself to confront fear isn't exploitative if I use it to reach out to others in an authentic way—it's exploitation's second cousin: usefulness.

There are people who spend their whole lives afraid; that is what I want to remember even as I try to exploit my own fear to make the world better. Fear can be sacred just because it witnessed an atrocity and had the courage to stay afraid. There are girls in basements who are scared of their captors, are brave, but then die in those basements. I think it's possible that some fear is simply bearing witness to that treachery. And that's all that they can do.

But fear, real and imagined, can be so very productive, as long as we choose to act anyway. They say it isn't bravery if you aren't scared. Fear should be a catalyst, not a position. Fear forces Jane to tell her sad tale to the doctor, who helps her find a way out. Fear can help our "soul [find] its deepest expression."* Empathic fear can make us interrupt things that those from within don't have the power to disrupt. Given that we are all afraid of such different things, fear is, after all, the only necessary ingredient for courage.

* Jan G. Gaarlandt, introduction to *An Interrupted Life: The Diaries and Letters of Etty Hillesum 1941–43* (London: Persephone Books, 1999).

CHAPTER THREE

On Commitment

I must keep in good health, and not die.

—Chapter 4, *Jane Eyre*

O n my first day of coursework at divinity school I attended a class with my entire cohort of fellow students pursuing their master of divinity degrees, called Introduction to Ministry Studies. If my memory serves me (it is a self-serving memory), the very first story in the very first lecture that I heard was given by Professor Stephanie Paulsell.

The story she told is about a town in France called Le Chambon-sur-Lignon. This town was made up of Huguenots—Protestants in an otherwise Catholic country—who, after generations of being violently and socially oppressed, dedicated themselves to the idea of radical hospitality. They took the legacy of hundreds of years of institutional betrayal and violence and cashed it in for a practice of risk and remarkable virtue. They built false doors and kept extra food and linens for any guest who might come and need hiding or a refuge. They were prepared to do whatever was necessary to welcome people who needed welcoming.

So when World War II revved up in France and the Vichy government began to round up Jews, Jews started knocking on the doors of the townspeople of Le Chambon-sur-Lignon. When the Nazi guards would come to look, the Jews were sent into the mountains to hide. A song was arranged as a signal for Jews to come out of their mountainous hiding spots and back to the safety of the town when the guards had left. Around a thousand Jews were saved through the efforts, sacrifice, and risk of these townspeople.

What is especially remarkable to me about this story is that the townspeople of Le Chambon-sur-Lignon made a commitment based on their experiences of oppression. When they made the commitment to radical hospitality, they did not know how history would play out; they did not know who would come knocking or what those people would need.

Commitments are always promises we shout into the unknown. We never really understand what it is that we are committing to. We agree to dinner with a friend, knowing that we believe in spending time with a loved one, but not knowing how we will feel that night, what the weather will be, what food we'll be in the mood for, or what the friend will want to talk about. We agree to get married knowing we love a person, knowing we can envision a life with them, but having no idea what life will throw at us. Lord knows children come into our lives and we have no idea who they will become, but we commit to loving them nonetheless.

These commitments are made because we don't know. They are an admission of a lack of control and an attempt to regain control of our identities. Commitments can be freeing. They allow us to focus on one thing rather than look around at everything, including at the abyss. If we make plans for dinner with a friend, it means we aren't going to write the next great song that night. But it also means we are saved from the potential despair of chaos.

Commitments are also only as good as the follow-through. Many were committed to the idea of radical hospitality prior to World War II, including the United States, which asks for the tired, poor, huddled masses yearning to breathe free and yet turned away the MS *St. Louis*, sending nine hundred Jews back to Europe and all but certain death in 1939. Follow-through is everything.

I am naturally skeptical of commitment. I think I am more

afraid of it than ever these days. I just came off of being ill for two years and had to cancel on one particular friend six times in a row. These were plans made each and every time in good faith. But my body kept me home.

Even since before I got sick, however, holding things loosely seems a virtue to me on a day-to-day basis. I can look at my partner and tell him that he is the most important thing to me, but then one of my parents can get sick and I will abandon him to go back to California and be with them. Anything can be taken away, and promises that I have made with every intention of not just follow-through, but A-plus follow-through, have had to be broken, sometimes for good reason and sometimes because I "had" to go to bed early. So, as enraptured as I was with the Hugenots of Le Chambon-sur-Lignon and their masterful commitment to an idea realized in actual saved lives, I knew myself better than that and wondered: What if the person who needs refuge under my roof is annoying? What if the day someone comes knocking, I just don't want to let them in?

Very little in my life is precious. My family has no heirlooms, for obvious reasons, and the few we've sort of made were stolen by a relative, for trauma reasons if I'm being generous, and asshole reasons if I'm a little hangry. So I came to the disposition that it's best not to care too much. Best not to be precious about much.

I know how dead inside this sounds. But in my defense, the commitments that I saw were confusing. My parents are utterly devoted to each other, granted. But Papa, my mother's father, was committed to a detachment that was pathological. He left his keys in the ignition of his unlocked car his entire American life, no matter how many cars were stolen or who was inconvenienced (sometimes it wasn't his car whose keys he left sitting there). When he was arrested by the Gestapo the first time, his father (my great-grandfather) bailed my Papa out of jail. Papa opted to stay in jail an extra night because it was movie night and he didn't want to miss the movie. In jail. I don't want to be so committed to fatalism that I'd stay in prison another night to enjoy a movie.

Of course, in his defense, Papa's commitment to being detached, to not caring, was bred within him. He was brutally beaten by his mother growing up; the beatings were so bad that sometimes she wouldn't let him go to school the next day because she was embarrassed by the wounds she had inflicted on him. And he would defend her as a great mother until his dying day. That was trauma separate from the concentration camps.

So of course he became detached from the impact of his choices and began doing things like cheating on Mama, with her friends, neighbors, community members, and his employees. But then he took painstaking care of my grandmother from the moment she was bedridden until the last day of her life. He bought her bra extenders, and I'd imagine that even at eighty years old he flirted with the salesclerks at Macy's. Even though he thought religion was dumb, he went to temple twice a day for a year after Mama died to say the mourner's prayer. But then (just the last flip-flop) we moved him into a smaller apartment, and he started dating the most convenient woman around, his downstairs neighbor. She, it turned out, formerly had Nazi ties.

After about the first twenty pages of *Jane Eyre*, in which all we read about is the abuse and neglect the ten-year-old Jane suffers at the hands of her aunt and cousins, the formal verbal and physical abuse stops, and she enters into an emotional abuse of active, intentional neglect. She is ignored for months in the huge mansion Gateshead. The servants are on orders to serve her in an austere way but to otherwise avoid her. She is in complete isolation from Christmas until spring. Then one day, completely out of nowhere, she is beckoned to the living room to meet with Aunt Reed. Her face and hands are scrubbed by a maid and Jane is sent down for unknown reasons. In addition to Aunt Reed, a man named Mr. Brocklehurst is there. He and Jane are introduced.

It is then made clear that Aunt Reed has arranged for Jane to be sent away to Mr. Brocklehurst's school, the Lowood

Institution, and that Aunt Reed has already given Mr. Brocklehurst an intentionally false and damning report on Jane's character with the seeming intention of continuing to abuse Jane even when she is no longer in her aunt's care. Mr. Brocklehurst presents as thrilled at the idea of a child to punish and does not waste a second with any pleasantries or explanations. One of the first questions he asks Jane is, "What is hell? Can you tell me that?" She replies with orthodoxy, "A pit full of fire."

He then asks what she must do to avoid spending eternity there. She responds with one of my favorite lines in all of literature: "I must keep in good health, and not die."

Jane obviously isn't saying that she thinks she can beat death. She is being combative and hilarious, granted. She is on some level simply trying to avoid giving these horrible people what they want: a cowering, bullied reply of, "Everything I can to please you."

I think part of what Jane is saying is, "I will do my best to stay in good health until I can die a different person than I am now." I don't think she is saying that she thinks she needs to change from the inside, but that her circumstances need to change. What Jane is committing to is trying to survive. And sometimes survival is sufficient.

Jane is also at the beginning of developing her own theology and rejecting the theology of Aunt Reed and Brocklehurst, who are looking to the next life, the great beyond, for meaning. But Jane is looking to this world, to the future she believes is in this world and therefore can be lived into reality. She is demanding justice in this life.

The kinds of commitments, for the most part, that I am asked to make are to my partner, to my friends, to my family, and to my work. These commitments are sometimes a lot on my mere mortal soul. I am almost always disappointing someone, and it haunts me. But the commitments that I hold are, by and large, wonderful challenges and are mostly easy, if not to rise to, at least to wrap my head around. So the question that I'm struggling with here isn't what do I want to do in my pedestrian, everyday commitments but in extreme circumstances.

What do I want to practice on a daily basis to help ground me in the extreme circumstances? When the seas rise and water runs out, when there is a pandemic and no cure, what do I want to commit myself to then? Do I want to keep my commitments small, a fair and noble position? Or do I want to be Le Chambon-sur-Lignon?

There have been many times in my life when I have felt strongly that if someone would simply tell me the right thing to do, I would find the strength to rise up and do it. Jane's commitment is to survive Aunt Reed's and Brocklehurst's torment of her. But her commitment is also to find a more just world for herself—a world in which she doesn't have to look to the next life but can have enough satisfaction in this one to then be ready to look beyond.

I want my commitments to be one-size-fits-all, to be what is right when confronted with Brocklehursts, to be what I would do for a friend who had a bad day and what I would do under the threat of the Nazis. I know this sounds extremist or lazy. But what I am going for is practiced. I want to be working up to the big goal of being the person I want to be in difficult moments. And so my commitments have to be consistent so I can practice now for the big day. The people of Le Chambon-sur-Lignon had that. In all those circumstances, the commitment stayed the same: radical hospitality.

Jane's commitment starts so small. She ends up being a woman of incredible integrity, one who will pity when she could judge and who will forgive the unforgivable. And all she commits to practicing is "I must not die." Which makes me wonder if promising to try to survive is actually enough.

I used to marvel at my grandparents' will to survive. They were surrounded for years by electric fences, inviting them into a suicidal embrace. I believe that Virginia Woolf's suicide was a war death; she knew her name was on a list of those to be rounded up when Germany invaded Britain, and when she killed herself in 1941, the German invasion looked more like a certainty than like a distinct possibility. And I respect her for walking into a river with stones in her pockets.

I never thought survival for its own sake is a virtue. But it is the only commitment that Jane makes, and it makes me wonder, what is it, exactly, that I wouldn't be willing to survive in order to see what's on the other side?

It is important for me to hold on to the notion that certain things aren't worth surviving. If I were to get a terminal diagnosis full of pain, I think I'd opt to leave this earth rather than suffer and burden the people around me. I do not judge those who opt not to survive. And I especially do not judge those who simply did not survive.

I have been told many times that my grandparents are heroes. They weren't heroes for their survival. Survival does not reward the deserving or the noble. Survival is almost entirely just luck. If you're born white in America, if your water isn't poisoned, if the bridge collapses ten minutes after you drive over it, if you get cancer now instead of one hundred years ago, all you are is luckier than the ones who didn't survive.

Papa survived because on the day his bunker was taken to the gas chambers, he had volunteered to go to the mail room, where they were short on Russians due to a disease coming through the Russian bunker. That was one of the times he was lucky. Lucky. Not heroic.

What broke within my grandparents that allowed them to withstand what they went through? The answers I have come to are not that they didn't make any compromises and survived with all of their humanity intact. But it is a tempting line of questioning: Is there something wrong with those of us who survive? Survival is not a virtue.

But Jane is making me wonder if survival, even if it is not a virtue, can be a commitment worth making. For the first time, I realize that my grandparents' commitment to survival does deserve one of many forms of respect. It is hard to remember that surviving—the persistence of it, the grit of it—is a miracle when 7.5 billion people live on earth. But only 13 percent of prisoners in Auschwitz survived. The Nazis didn't fail. They got a B+. Even amid despair, one of the things motivating my grandparents to keep going had to be similar to Jane's: "I will try not to die on *your* terms." And another component has to be a belief in the future. Why survive if you believe that the rest of your life will be like this? A willingness to survive is about believing in the possibility of a better future. Survival is about hope, and hope in moments of despair is virtuous. Jane standing in front of two adults who want to oppress her and saying, "I will survive," is an act of commitment to hope.

"I will survive," said by a person with less power to a person with more power, is also a threat to the status quo. "I will survive" is a promise of change. As the wellness industry co-opts the idea of self-care and capitalism tries to turn our bodies into constant productivity machines, maybe "I will survive" is the commitment we all should be making. We need to take care of ourselves enough to survive with the fire within us intact. We need to survive in order to witness and in order to be agents of change. We need to believe that wanting to survive is at times enough, because we are enough. Surviving as a commitment may sound like a low bar to jump. But sometimes you need the bar to be low so that you can gather up the strength to once again clear higher ones.

On Being In Between

The present was vague and strange, and of the future
I could form no conjecture.

—Chapter 5, *Jane Eyre*

O n my first day of my new kindergarten I was handed a
sheet of paper. The teacher took it from me and used a
rubber stamp to emboss the word *Homework* on the top of the
sheet. That is the first time I remember an overwhelming wave
of dread hitting me.

On my eighth birthday I got exactly what I wanted: beautiful
drawing paper and a set of stunning colored pencils, sharpened
and ready for use. I sat at my desk and felt miserable. I drew a
self-portrait of that misery and hid it. I hated myself for not
being happy on my birthday. I remember thinking, "I'm a kid.
It's weird to not be happy as a kid."

When I was twelve I counted each day of school left from our big calendar and spent an hour cutting up notecards into tiny pieces and numbering them until the mid–one hundreds (the number of school days left). Five mornings a week, I would get to trash the number that corresponded to yesterday's day of school. Another one down. Friday afternoons were bliss for me. But by Saturday morning I was already hopeless at the thought that another week was ahead of me. I would cry through my younger brother's Saturday morning soccer games, miserable at the prospect of Monday.

At fifteen I couldn't get myself to go to school. I would plead with my mother, "Tomorrow, please," and she would somehow acquiesce. I had a good part in the school play. I wanted to go to school to go to rehearsal, the only part of my day that I enjoyed. But I didn't. I couldn't. After I'd missed a week of school, my drama teacher, Ms. Lyons, called me at home. My mom answered and forced me to get on the phone. After the pleasantries, Ms. Lyons asked, "Vanessa. Are you depressed?" and I immediately started crying. Yes. Depressed. But it was the nineties. We didn't know what to do with that word. So I went back to school the next day. The thing was at least named. That helped.

All through college my roommates had to deal with me falling asleep to DVDs that I played on my computer on my desk, across the bedroom. The music from a DVD of *Sex and the City* would play for hours after the episodes had run through and gone back to the menu screen, until I woke up, stomped across the room to press "play all" again, and went back into my bed to listen to the show until I fell asleep again. I once said that I liked falling asleep to *Friends* more than *Sex and the City* and my roommate said, "Because *Friends* just plays on loop and doesn't get stuck on the menu?" Yes. That was it. She preferred that as well, she didn't say.

Sometimes the depression took on the form of tremendous physical pain. Aching, spasms, headaches. Mostly the physical manifestation was exhaustion.

But then there was a time when I was twenty-two. I was happily living with my best friend and across the hall from two more friends and paying $425 a month for a gorgeous apartment in Clayton, Missouri. I had just graduated from college and was gleefully writing and waitressing and nannying, running from one thing to the next. I saved dollars in an old red makeup bag that was cracking on the inside, and I would try to make clear to the teller at the bank that I wasn't a stripper even though all my money was in ones and fives, while simultaneously not trying to denigrate strippers, whom I totally supported. I had just finished writing a play that I am miraculously, fifteen years later, not entirely humiliated by, when a depression hit. I chanted to myself, "Function. Function. Function." But the chant couldn't get me into the shower. It got me to a low weight because I ate only one bowl of Honey Nut Cheerios a day. My mom flew out to get me and we drove home to L.A. It was time to do something about this.

I'll never forget the man who diagnosed me. He was hunched over, bent at a forty-five-degree angle. And he said, "I have good news; you're not interesting at all. You're textbook," and sent me home with a pill pack that would gently increase my dose over the course of six weeks.

I've been on slight variations of that same medication ever since. Depressions still hit, but I feel them from a distance. And Netflix, blessedly, knows about depression so asks, "Are you still watching? Or did your depression pull you back into the sweet relief of slumber?" So even when I have my gentler versions of the swell, at least the technology is better.

Now the depressions are echoes, shallow. But every time a full-blown episode used to hit me, it took me by surprise and then immediately felt familiar, like that great molasses disaster. Something coming on fast, in order for me to be stuck in slowness.

It takes a short while to organize things enough to get Jane out of the Reeds' house. But after the visit from Mr. Brockle-hurst, Aunt Reed finally gets what she wants: Jane gets cast out of the Reed mansion of Gateshead. Jane goes to the Lowood school, run by Mr. Brocklehurst, and the school is told that she is not to come back to Gateshead for vacations of any sort; Lowood is her new, full-time home.

Jane travels by carriage from Gateshead to Lowood alone. She arrives and is stripped of her quality clothes, then put in a smock that matches the other girls' uniforms. After less than twelve hours at Lowood, she is still overwhelmed and confused. She has barely said a word. But she has gotten a rough sense of her new surroundings. She has observed that the place is run on discipline and routine. She's seen that Miss Temple is kind. She knows that the food is often inedible, and when it is edible it is not enough to fill her up.

Even though it is a cold January day, the children are sent out for time in the small garden, and Jane, trying to wrap herself tighter and tighter in her too-thin clothes, stands still in a corner and is given her first chance to think and reflect. Until this moment she has been moved from room to room, activity to activity, and has been kept so busy that she has just been trying to keep up. But now that she has a moment to stop, she notices that "I hardly yet knew where I was; Gateshead and my past life seemed floated away to an immeasurable distance; the present was vague and strange, and of the future I could form no conjecture."

I was a proctor at Harvard University for seven years, which meant that I lived in the dorms with freshmen. I watched them arrive at college, hurried, glazed, anxious. They either had generations of family members' glory to live up to, or they were the first in their family to come to Harvard. Their childhoods were immeasurable distances in the past, but their futures were still entirely unclear. After years of having exacting routines, they were thrust into a totally new situation. And they each handled it so differently—some patiently, some eagerly.

Jane stays still, waiting for the present to unfold. She reminds me of my most shocked students: the ones from remote countries who had just got off their first airplanes and could fathom neither the snow that would be on the ground in two months nor the difference between professors and teaching assistants. I had a student from near the equator who kept locking himself out of his room (the doors locked automatically behind the students) because he was from an area in the world without locks. He also couldn't fathom why he had been given five hundred dollars for winter gear. I had to explain boots *and* a coat, *and* a hat, *and* gloves. He had a past that had floated away to an immeasurable distance and a future that he could form no conjecture of. I knew both of those things, but I'm not sure I realized that, most likely, as with Jane, it wasn't just that he wasn't sure of his past or his future but that his present was also vague.

It's such an odd thing for your present to be vague. We talk about mindfulness, about counting your breaths, feeling your feet on the floor below you, and being "in the moment." But that isn't the same thing as knowing what is going on. If your present is vague, it means that you are seeing what is in front of you, are witnessing what is transpiring, and are entirely in your body. It means that you are all of those things but that you still cannot understand what you're witnessing. This is shock. Jane, in this scene, is in shock. She is entirely in her body—cold, hungry, absorbing everything through her observant eyes and trying her best to categorize it. But she doesn't know what she is seeing.

Those moments in a depression are the most jarring: when I am already depressed, but can remember caring. I'll look at an open magazine on a table and think, "Just yesterday, I cared about what that page had to say." And yet my caring yesterday seems an immeasurable distance away. Usually the magazine will stay open to that page for days, if not weeks. But the future, in these moments, seems even harder to grasp. I know that the depression will pass, from years of experience. But it seems not only impossible in that moment but unwanted. If I have a future, then this feeling that I am having right now is less true. And it feels *so true* when I am having it. My future is mocking my present.

One of the strangest things about depression is that it is simultaneously a deeply unhealthy way to walk through the world but it is also in many ways truer than not being depressed. When depressed, I see the world more clearly than I do when I am not. I am not depressed as I type this. But I really do think that my depressed thoughts are truer; I am despondent about the future (which in a climate-changed world is simply fair). Abstractly, I know that people love me, but I also know that, aside from a few people, my disappearance wouldn't matter. I see people as essentially selfish, which is using my own instincts as the model. And I dread feeling better, because I know that all feeling better actually is is a chemical state of distraction. A healthy chemical state of distraction, but one nonetheless. And yet, I recite the platitude, "This too shall pass," not to assuage my distress, but to allow myself to revel in the depression. "Enjoy this misery. For it too shall pass."

> "Enjoy this misery. For it too shall pass."

Depression, for me, is like Jane standing outside on her first day at Lowood; it is a freezing cold place for frank reflection. It is a liminal space, a space most notable for being between other places, where yesterday's life seems impossibly far away and yet a future is unimaginable. And so the present is as isolated as it can possibly be. Airports are liminal spaces, places you would never go for themselves but only in order to go elsewhere. Waiting rooms at doctors' offices are another example. And there is little more grotesque to us than when a liminal space becomes a permanent one. We abhor it and litigate against it: bus benches cannot be beds; cars cannot be homes. Those are for in between, not for the long term.

When I was a child we went to my grandparents' house every Friday night for Shabbat dinner. They lived about six miles from us, in Northridge, California. One Friday in January 1994 we went over as usual for Shabbat dinner. Mama, my grandmother, asked me to get her a pencil and paper. I walked over to this odd-looking pencil holder that was red and had spongelike talons sticking out from it and took a pencil. I grabbed a pad of paper that was a promotional pad from a real estate agent. When she was done, I put both pencil and pad back.

Monday afternoon, less than seventy-two hours later, we were over at my grandparents', cleaning up after the Northridge earthquake, the one that is still the highest ever recorded on an instrument in an urban area in North America. Their refrigerator was on the other side of the room from the wall where it belonged. And I found the pencil holder, not neatly filled with pencils and sitting proudly by the phone, but on the floor on the other side of the room.

My grandparents' house after the earthquake felt liminal on that Monday afternoon—like it was a mess, but we would get it back to its normal shape. We'd move the fridge back, and I even put the pencil holder back myself.

But that newly and quickly created space ended up not being liminal at all. The earthquake changed everything. The house was forever changed. It was not liminal; it was a new reality. Although my grandmother would live for another ten years, the earthquake (she broke her ankle during it) began her more rapid demise. The house was never returned to its previous glory. We stopped going there for Shabbat dinners. That Friday night with the pencil was our last one at that house with the whole big family. My childhood ended with that earthquake.

Everything can always be normal on Friday and destroyed on Monday. Jane was just a carriage ride away from her new reality. And these types of destruction can be highly local. Although I went to middle school only twenty miles away, it wasn't on the fault line we were on. So although we looked like we lived in a bombed-out city in a World War II movie, my school counted me as truant for not attending. And the change for Jane was so local that her cousins, who had lived in the same house with her since she was a year old, did not share her fate.

Jane, in this moment in the garden, when her present is vague, is realizing that this liminal space will be her new life.

She is getting accustomed to that realization and trying to figure out what it is that she is looking at, what the rules are here. Richard Rohr, an author and Franciscan priest, says that being in a liminal space, such as Jane's wintry garden at Lowood, is "when you have left the tried and true, but have not yet been able to replace it with anything else. It is when you are between your old comfort zone and any possible new answer."

But Jane stays. She keeps looking around her, trying to take it in. She reads the inscription carved into the wall of the building, over and over. She doesn't run; she stays stock-still, reading and rereading, trying to make a kind of sense of what is in front of her. The cough of a nearby girl draws her out of her state; that girl will end up being Helen Burns, Jane's first true friend in the world.

Jane, by not running but by staying still, is invited into the next moment. Liminal spaces are places of pain and discomfort. But they are also, most importantly, invitations. We often want to skip the in-between. Go from one relationship to another, have a job lined up before we graduate from school. But the in-between is the place to see where you are, assess, and decide with intention where you are going next.

CHAPTER FIVE

On Kindness

I came on purpose to find you, Jane Eyre.

—Chapter 8, *Jane Eyre*

In November 1970, my father came to Los Angeles from Holon, Israel. He had just gotten out of the Israeli army, where he had fought in the Six-Day War, on the front line. His father figured the country of Israel wasn't big enough for my dad and my dad's mom (Anyu) to peacefully coexist. I also suspect that my grandfather, after experiencing Auschwitz and communism, found Israel to be the only place he ever wanted to live, but he wanted something bigger for my dad. So my grandfather arranged for my dad to go to Australia as a photographer's apprentice for a year. I imagine my grandfather was hoping that my father would find a life, a passion, and maybe even something that would keep him away. He loved my father that much.

On his way to Australia, my dad stayed in Los Angeles for a few weeks. My mom and dad met at a dinner party. My mom got assigned to show my dad around for the few days he was set to be in town. Then my dad got sick. Really sick. Mono turned into hepatitis. The family he was staying with, worried about an elderly person in the house, kicked out my dad. Papa took my dad in. When I asked my dad how this happened, what exactly had been said, he replied, "It was never explicitly discussed. You know Papa. It was just . . . done."

This is a story I know the contours of well. It's how my parents had the chance to fall in love. But no matter the reason that my father tells the story, he always includes one detail. He will tell you that each night that he was staying in Mama, Papa, and my mom's house while he was sick, Papa would come home from work, immediately come into the room where my dad was staying, and feel his forehead, checking for fever. Papa would do this with his suit jacket still over his arm. He wouldn't even stop to hang up his jacket before he would come and check on my dad. *Tender* is the word my dad uses.

My father tells this story of his future father-in-law as a love story. He didn't just fall in love with my mom in those weeks in Los Angeles but with Papa as well. My father doesn't know the details of how he ended up at my mother's house. You always just take everyone in, if you're my father. But to come first thing after a long day of work and check the strange boy's forehead, even before you've hung up your suit jacket . . . that made an impression. That is kindness. And kindness is something different altogether.

We know that *kind* is a good word and *nice* is not quite as good a word. George Saunders, in the famous graduation speech he gave at Syracuse, said, "What I regret most in my life are failures of kindness." And to me there is such wisdom in that. Politeness matters, because it is a gesture toward the humanity of people you are treating transactionally and it acknowledges a lack of entitlement. You are polite to a waiter as a gesture, as if you are saying, "I know that I will never know your full story, so instead I will say please and thank you." You say please to your parents because they make sacrifices beyond your comprehension, and really you say please and thank you to your parents either as training for the outside world or to demonstrate to them how you behave when they aren't looking.

Niceness, to some extent, is actually self-serving, right? Not in a bad way. Timothy Snyder, in his brilliant screed *On Tyranny*, argues positively for living in the position of niceness as a way to fight against fascism. He says that making eye contact and small talk is "not just polite . . . It is also a way to stay in touch with your surroundings, break down social barriers, and understand whom you should and should not trust." Snyder notes that across memoirs of people who describe living in moments of rising fascism, when neighbors stopped saying hello to each other, the more vulnerable population knew that times were getting unsafe.

It costs almost nothing to be nice. Saying "You have a nice day too" to the person at CVS costs nothing and makes the days go by swifter. And I think Snyder makes a compelling argument on the importance of being nice. He ends this chapter with two brilliant sentences: "Having old friends is the politics of last resort. And making new ones is the first step toward change."

Snyder argues that niceness, with all its limitations, in some circumstances is actually a way to fight tyranny.

Tyranny reigns at the Lowood school, Jane's new home. Older girls steal food from the younger girls because none of them get enough to fill their bellies. A teacher beats a student for not cleaning her fingernails, when in fact the wash basins' water was frozen during bath time in the morning. Students faint on Sundays, due to the rigor of the Lord's day, unable to endure the marathon of walking in freezing weather and standing in the position of prayer. On the Sabbath even the teachers are "too much dejected to attempt the task of cheering others."

The tyranny seems to be run by an absent force. Jane has been at Lowood for three weeks before Mr. Brocklehurst, the man who had visited her at the Reeds' house and asked what hell was like, the headmaster of Lowood, comes to visit. His visit shows him to be the embodiment of debasement and arbitrary abuse of power.

After Jane's response to him at Gateshead, that she would survive him, he had informed her that he would tell everyone at Lowood that she is a liar. Although she has been starved and frozen for weeks, what she has been dreading is Brocklehurst's coming and fulfilling his promise to tell Miss Temple and everyone else there about Jane's "vicious nature."

Jane tries and fails to hide from Brocklehurst, hoping that if he doesn't see her, he won't remember to discredit her. She knows that, to him, ruining her reputation would be nothing more than an afterthought that would please him, while for her the impact of his afterthought would be living in a place that not only is less comfortable than her aunt's house, but has the same negative impression of her. Cruelty costs the giver so little effort, but costs the victim much trauma. Jane tries desperately to hide, knowing how little she truly matters to this man.

But her slate falls from her fingers and makes a loud crash. So he notices her and calls her forward, saying, "It is the new pupil,

I perceive [who broke her slate]. I must not forget I have a word to say respecting her." He then has Jane stand on a stool and tells all the teachers, students, and servants in the room that while Jane possessed "the ordinary form of childhood . . . the Evil One had already found a servant and agent" in her. He then instructs Jane to stay standing on the stool for half an hour and tells her fellow students to permanently "avoid her company" and the teachers to "'punish her body to save her soul."

Jane is mortified by this. Helen Burns, the young girl whose cough Jane notices while standing in the garden, reaches out to her; Helen smiles at her while still on the stool even though all the other girls are too scared to do so. When Jane is allowed down from the stool, she cries to Helen, saying that she is ruined, that now all the other girls must hate her, thinking that she is a liar and an instrument of the devil. Helen counters, telling Jane that in fact, "As it is, the greater number would offer you sympathy if they dared."

The "if they dared" is incredible. It announces the difference between the neighbors who say hello when we live in peace and those who stop when tyranny is on the rise. "If they dared" is the beginning of the difference between niceness or politeness and kindness. Kindness requires sacrifice. Kindness requires a form of courage. Kindness is niceness that survives a tyrannical monster—and can at times even slay it.

Part of why we love Jane is because she admits to the frailty of being human. In talking to Helen, she says, "If others don't love me, I would rather die." She admits that her own good opinion of herself is not enough. It is this vulnerability that we love in

Kindness requires a form of courage.

Jane. We love that she will later describe herself as "poor, obscure, plain, and little." We are invited to see ourselves in her because she isn't perfect. When Helen tells her that she is not hated, and that in fact if Mr. Brocklehurst came in and sang her praises, she would be despised, Jane needs that buoying, but it is not enough. Luckily, Miss Temple comes to find Jane.

"I came on purpose to find you, Jane Eyre," Miss Temple says. Again, the "on purpose" is important for kindness. It is not kindness if it is accidental. Kindness is brave and it is with intention. Miss Temple says she would like to have Jane come to her private office and talk to her, but then she adds that since Helen is with Jane, Helen should come as well. Helen being invited "as well" is a perfect foil for niceness versus kindness. By Helen coming, an allyship is further formed between her and Jane. But also, Helen, who it turns out is sick, is given loving attention from the pillar of goodness of Miss Temple. It is *good* that Miss Temple includes Helen Burns. It just does not meet the rigors of what it is to be kind; it is the right advantage taking of an opportunity, and beautiful and trained and wise. But it is not *kind*.

Miss Temple has just been told to brutalize Jane and instead is singling her out positively. She is putting herself at risk; there are obvious spies at the school, who report back to Mr. Brocklehurst and will tell him that Miss Temple did the opposite of what he demanded. Miss Temple could lose her position, her home, and her livelihood. Most likely she will not, but she absolutely could. She invites Jane and Helen up to her chambers anyway.

Once up in in her private rooms, Miss Temple gives Jane the chance to express her concerns and despair. Jane shares that she is despondent over the fact that her peers and teachers will now think her evil, which is a false report. Miss Temple tells Jane that no, "we shall think you what you prove yourself to be, my child," and then instructs Jane to give her own side of the story, advising, "Say whatever your memory suggests is true; but add nothing and exaggerate nothing."

Jane tells the story of her abuse and neglect at Gateshead as simply and calmly as she can. She then reports, "I felt as I went on that Miss Temple truly believed me." Miss Temple says that she will send a letter to a potentially corroborating witness of Jane's story. She knows that her personally believing Jane isn't enough. She knows that she has a reputation for being kind-hearted, which will sway the other teachers away from believing her instinct about Jane. So she puts forth effort in writing a letter to present facts to back her instinct.

Miss Temple then no longer treats the two girls as if she has business with them, but instead says, "You two are my visitors tonight; I must treat you as such." She tries to get provisions from the kitchen to have tea with them, but the cook, with the tyrannical mind-set firmly in place, says that the usual amount of provisions was sent up and will not send up any more. So although Miss Temple was going to send the two girls back to their rooms with pieces of seed cake that she had received as a gift, she instead gives them hearty slices now. She takes the transactional experience of meeting with a student and turns it into the breaking of bread, into communion.

I think that true kindness is in all of these components. Say hi to your neighbors to fight tyranny, but be kind to continue to fan the flames of humanity within yourself. True kindness must be brave, it must be intentional, it must include sacrifice, and it absolutely must entirely humanize the other and ourselves.

George Saunders knows this. He does not hold regrets of cruelty. Most of us are not cruel. But in a commencement speech at Kenyon College, he says that what he regrets is "those moments when another human being was there, in front of me, suffering, and I responded . . . sensibly. Reservedly. Mildly." Kindness is bold and vulnerable. It is not and cannot be sensible.

My grandfather was just as at risk of contracting hepatitis as my father's other friends were. And yet he didn't just take my father in, he tenderly felt his forehead. The kindness of Papa does not match the kindness of Miss Temple. But it speaks to the same idea that we can always be doing a little more to be as human as possible to each other, like Jane is to us by telling us a version of her story that does not glorify herself, but invites us in. God sets this precedent in the telling of the Passover story. Jews each year say, "Dayenu," which translates to "It would have been enough," but God gives more. Kindness is an opportunity to be godlike. To not only ask for another account of the story, but to send a follow-up letter asking for proof. To not only let the sick boy into your house, but to go feel his forehead as soon as you get home.

CHAPTER SIX

On Destiny

A kind fairy, in my absence, had surely dropped the
required suggestion on my pillow.

—Chapter 10, *Jane Eyre*

I don't remember where we were. Walking from somewhere to somewhere else. We were probably walking pretty slowly and we were probably arm in arm, because Papa was already quite elderly. Ninety at least.

I also don't remember what I had said that made him say this to me; probably something overly simplistic and dumb. But one day, Papa said to me, "You should be grateful for the Holocaust. You wouldn't be here without it." The only thing I remember about the rest of the conversation is that I replied at some point, "I'm not sure that's how it works."

I don't know what he meant by that comment, really. But I cannot imagine that he looked at me, a true product of the Holocaust, who wouldn't exist in any way without it, and thought: Worth it. I don't think he did the moral calculus. The closest I can get to a theory is that he really thought I was so removed from the Holocaust that I could be grateful for it because I now had this life. Which, given the life that he inadvertently helped provide for me, sort of makes sense. I also think he was making a joke. All this is to say I think he meant it and that he didn't.

But if we take him at face value—which was almost always a mistake with Papa—then what he was saying was: "You were destined to exist and the Holocaust was part of that process to get you here." Which, while untrue, is an important idea to grapple with, because it is a logic that is built into the way we think, the decisions we make, and even the language we use. "Everything will be fine," people like to say. It isn't true. Everything will be; things will unfold. But everything definitely will not be fine.

I don't believe in destiny. I can't. If I did, I'd have to believe that my grandparents were destined to go through hell and I was destined to experience privilege. I am obsessed with stories of kidnapped women, from Elizabeth Smart to the Chibok schoolgirls kidnapped by Boko Haram. And I am obsessed with them in a highly problematic way: I don't want any tenet I live my life by to exclude them. So in trying to carry them with me, I of course objectify them and reduce them to their victimhood.

Destiny, it seems to me, is the belief of the lucky or the desperate. I think we can make meaning of our hardships; we can be grateful for the lessons we have learned through them and the people we have met because of them without being grateful for the hardships themselves.

Happily married people believe they were destined to find each other. Only a truly depressed, self-loathing person (who I believe is entitled to love and outreach) believes that they are destined to be lonely if they do not choose to be alone. In fact, a psychiatrist would probably diagnose such a person's belief in destiny as some sort of disorder. Psychologists certainly diagnose those who believe they are destined for too high a level of greatness. Believing in destiny seems to be a sickness of kings, like gout. I want to get rich without the destiny belief—or gout.

So the luckier I get, the more I want to hold on to my belief in the arbitrary nature of things, in a confluence of luck and a few choices plus personality, privilege, and circumstance. It is important to me not to believe in destiny as long as there are still girls in basements, men in prison, and trans people being discriminated against for who they are.

One cannot sum up Jane's exact theology or summarize her

beliefs in the novel. They are unclear because the story takes place over about twenty years and her beliefs change over the course of her life, which is, of course, a good thing. She contradicts herself regularly. One of the most quoted lines from the novel is: "I would always rather be happy than dignified." Its popularity frustrates me. Jane says it more than a hundred pages and many traumatizing incidents after she says, "Laws and principles are not for the times when there is no temptation: they are for moments such as this; when body and soul rise in mutiny against their rigour." She nearly starves to death between these two sentiments. Of course, I understand why people pull out the quote as inspiration. We should learn from the conclusions that our heroes come to, not the silly thoughts that they have moved past. I get annoyed because I want all the context around the statement. The lesson of choosing happiness over dignity is one that Jane earns, and I, without wishing suffering upon anyone, believe that we all have to earn it a little. Besides, how do we know that Jane still feels this way twenty years after the book ends? She might, after years of comfort, choose dignity again.

As far as we can pin it down, her personal theology seems to be, at minimum, a jumble of things. She painstakingly draws Judeo-Christian angels and talks of pagan fairies and sprites. She doesn't believe in fine clothing when it is Rochester who will foot the bill, but when we see her come into her own money, she realizes that it wasn't the nice clothes she objected to but someone else buying them for her. Jane learns about herself, and her beliefs evolve with her.

The novel is therefore a little murky on the grand ideas of destiny and fate. When Jane finds herself in the situation that leads to her nearly starving to death, she—completely by luck—ends up on the doorstep of people who turn out (hundreds of pages later) to be her cousins who she never knew existed. This seems to be a clear argument for believing in some kind of fate. Jane acts purely, relying on her principles to guide her, to be rewarded with shelter, food, and family.

But there are other moments in the text when it is clear that Jane does not believe in fate. She does not think it was fated that Aunt Reed be so awful to her. Jane believes that had her uncle lived, she would have had a comfortable childhood in which she would not have gone to Lowood, become a governess, or met Rochester. She also believes that Aunt Reed chose to resent Jane so much and that she would have accepted her aunt's love if it had been offered. Fate and destiny are at play at certain times in the novel and gone at others.

What Jane and the novel seem to consistently believe in, however, is a little bit of magic.

We see this one everlasting belief revealed fairly early on in the book. Jane has finished her education at Lowood, which has been made much better after an audit of the abuses of the children. Several children died in a tuberculosis epidemic, including Jane's best friend, Helen. But the losses led to a great improvement in the quality of life for the remaining students. Jane ended up flourishing at Lowood so much that she was offered a teacher's position there and stayed on in that capacity for a few years after her schooling was over. She, after all, really had nowhere to go.

Eventually Miss Temple leaves Lowood to get married. Jane calls Miss Temple's new husband "destiny," for it is he who gets Jane to finally leave Lowood, by taking Miss Temple away from her. Because once Miss Temple is gone, Jane does not feel as though Lowood can be her home. So even though Jane still has nowhere to go, she realizes that she has to leave.

It is the very day that Miss Temple goes off with her new husband that Jane realizes that she must go too. Suddenly, Lowood feels like a prison and Jane feels like she has been sent to live in exile. When she had to be there and learn, and it kept her away from Gateshead and the Reeds, it was a necessity. When she was choosing to stay as a teacher, it was a fairly good life. But now that she is there for no other reason than because she has nowhere else to go, it is suffocating her. She has a sense of urgency in her need to leave and she starts to take action immediately.

She sets aside some time to give the problem of where she should go and how she should support herself some real thought. She waits until her roommate is snoring and she then lies down, gets up, and paces around their shared room, effectively alone. She lies down again, all the while thinking it through, where she can go next.

Jane, in part, wants what she wants because she finds that there is "no use wanting anything better." Her dreams are shackled. She spends no time fantasizing about the best possible options for what she can do next. She skips all dreams and goes straight to pragmatism.

For a long time, nothing comes to her; she simply gets up, lies down, and frets. Eventually she physically exhausts herself. And it is then that she figures out what to do next. How she reports it is that "a kind fairy, in my absence, had surely dropped the required suggestion on my pillow; for as I lay down, it came quietly and naturally to my mind."

What I love about this scene is that it is, to some extent, Jane's hard work that gets her to the idea that she needs. She literally paces herself to a good idea. As someone who is obsessed with walking and is similarly obsessed with meditating on the ways that women are locked up, the poetry of Jane being able to walk herself to an epiphany even while trapped in a small space with a woman snoring in the same room delights me. It is a brief pilgrimage of the mind that she goes on in this moment—one in which she is able to imagine herself out of her current cell.

There is precedent for this kind of internal, entirely imaginative pilgrimage. Teresa of Ávila, a sixteenth-century Carmelite nun who was trying to empower her fellow nuns in her convent in Spain during the height of the Inquisition, told the nuns that they could go on pilgrimages of the mind, to their interior castles. Because the nuns were not allowed to do the same types of devotional practices as their male colleagues, Teresa's idea of the ability to meditate one's way into all spiritual practices that really matter is a beautiful one.

But this promise, that all we really need can be conjured from within us, is complicated. I am worried about the idea that we don't need earthly things like the freedom to travel or pursue any career we want—while such ideas can give solace, or allow people like Jane to make bold practical decisions, they can also keep people complacent. Really, I wish that the nuns had had the power to throw the Catholic church over and become priests themselves if they wanted it. I worry that Teresa's invitation to explore one's interior castles is as much about placation as it is about empowerment. Spiritual escapes are empowering and important, but they are not enough to satisfy me.

And Jane, in this scene where magic comes to her aid, seems to embody the ability for the mind to go on this journey of the soul while literally, physically, hitting the walls of its freedom. She is able to pace her way to an epiphany of escape; it is an epiphany grounded in compromise but still has action as a necessary component.

The notion of working one's way to freedom (be it financial freedom, the freedom from discrimination that can come with certain kinds of success, or even behaving well enough to be let out of literal imprisonment "early") is a very American notion, that one minute you can be stuck in obscurity, and then you can work your way to a better destiny. And it is an alluring story. We, as a culture, want to hold on to it because it means that we hold our fates in our own hands. But we know that our fates are actually determined by, for example, whether there was lead in the paint in our homes when we were crawling around as children and putting our hands in our mouths more than it will ever be determined by forty years of hard work. We have an American idea that hard work is our destiny, and yet we know that is not true. We know it isn't always the deserving who win. And we know that often the lazy and truly terrible thrive.

So what I really love about Jane having a fairy leave her the solution that she has been waiting for is that the hard work is necessary, but it is not enough. At the end of the day, it isn't even luck. It is something that cannot be explained at all.

At twenty-two, I was the assistant character in *The Devil Wears Prada* for a year. My monster of a boss, as he was taking off for a flight from Milwaukee, told me he needed something notarized that night. It was already five in the evening in Milwaukee as I frantically called from New York to find a notary. I called about thirty places; nowhere in the city would notarize after five p.m., but my boss insisted he needed it before nine o'clock the following morning. I called a Kinko's. The man told me, "You won't believe this but I just made business cards for the first twenty-four-hour notary in Wisconsin. Do you want the number?"

When my boss returned from Wisconsin, he preached on and on about what had happened as if it had been an allegory of his high demands and my hard work leading to us receiving our due. I remember staring at him and boiling with rage. Men with assistants can believe fate and hard work are a one-to-one ratio, I thought. But I knew the truth. It was a kind fairy.

Jane, from the beginning to the end of the book, believes in fairies. It is one of her few unchanging beliefs. She never *relies* on fairies. She only believes in them after the fact, after something good has already happened. So, granted, in this scene, she believes in fairies only after "forcing" her mind to think for hours, staring at stars, pacing, and enduring some decent insomnia. But she believes in fairies. The question becomes, what is a fairy?

Part of me wants to define a fairy by what it isn't. It isn't all the things that we believe actually cause destiny. Fairies are not hard work, money, luck, race, religion, gender, the time in which you're born, your health, inspiration, or whether there was lead in the paint when you were at the crawling age.

Fairies can be seduced, but they require consent. Fairies are our reasoned imaginings. The thing Jane imagines when she is trapped in the red room is that a ghost will come to her; that is the best she can conjure in that room. Now she is able to conjure an idea to get her out of Lowood into "a new servitude." The fairy does not leave her the idea of becoming a princess or a being of big adventures, as much as we know Jane longs for them. But it does present Jane with a leap. Fairies show us what is beyond the walls of wherever it is that we are trapped.

As committed as I am to my atheism, I don't want to be an atheist who thinks everything can be explained by science. Jane's fairies are my way back into contemplating destiny as a possibility to flirt with on occasion. Because I think fairies, reasonable imagination, can find their way into the basement where the Chibok girls are. And I think it's possible that as dire as Auschwitz was, some people there, for brief moments, whether

> ## Fairies can be seduced, but they require consent.
>
> ## Fairies are our reasoned imaginings.

or not they survived, had brief sightings of fairies. Fairies aren't destiny. Destiny is the man who took Miss Temple away. Destiny is the tanks that rolled in. Destiny is the big choices of people and systems. Fairies are the imagination that brings Jane the idea to search for a governess position by placing an advertisement in the paper. The life that Jane will live will be a negotiation between these powers and her fairies.

Not everyone can conjure fairies. Not only is it not their fault that they cannot conjure them, but they are to be applauded for not thinking of something as simple as fairies in places like Auschwitz, or prison, or abusive homes, or chemotherapy wards, or frankly, sometimes, just about anywhere on earth. But some people have access to fairies in the darkest of places. My grandparents survived death; I'm not sure whether they did it with or without the help of fairies.

I live with severe depression, and we know that trauma is inherited. I wonder if part of my depression is knowing that my existence hinges on such a horrible thing having happened. How can you be grateful for a life that was ill-gotten gains? I am the fruit of the poisonous tree. My fairies are all from Poland and bring me stories of women in basements. The patriarchy that is my destiny has been kind to me. But I need to keep pacing to conjure more and different kinds of fairies.

CHAPTER SEVEN

On Heartbreak

I can live alone, if self-respect and circumstances
require me so to do.

—Chapter 19, *Jane Eyre*

Jane gets herself a job at Thornfield Hall as a governess to a young French girl. It is here where she meets and becomes enchanted with her boss, Mr. Rochester.

When I read the novel for the first time, at fourteen years old, I fell in love with Mr. Rochester because I was supposed to fall in love with Mr. Rochester. I still love him, and I like to think that now it is, in part, for more complicated reasons. But partly, I think I still love him because I am supposed to. He is romantic; he is injured when we first meet him, and it turns out that he has demons as well. He is brooding, moody, and "complicated." He is exactly the kind of great, eccentric man that women are trained to endure and adore: the Dylans from *90210*, the Jesses from *Gilmore Girls*. Damaged men with hearts of gold are the dream young women are often taught. And I am no better than my training. But Mr. Rochester also cherishes Jane. He is fun and full of life. He is a deeply loving man. He is generous and strange. He's a catch.

Jane falls in love with Mr. Rochester at least in part because he has two traits that she has never experienced in a man before: he is there and he pays positive attention to her. Rochester's attention is not always kind, but it is acute. He looks at each of her drawings and paintings and does not compliment them other than to call them "odd." He really looks at her. He does not, as Mr. Brocklehurst or her cousin John Reed did, look at her as something to dominate, an object to humiliate. He looks at her to try to understand and connect with her. Jane falls in love with Rochester in large part because he is the first man to pay attention to her in a real way, and that attention feels like the sun shining on her. She does not realize that his attention is also a fire that could consume her.

And the more we get to know Rochester, the clearer it becomes that he is more than simply a man who is alive and noticing Jane. At the end of the novel, it turns out that Jane and Rochester can hear each other's voices on the wind, while hundreds of miles away from each other. After that supernatural moment, they find their way back to each other and achieve perfect bliss together. Call it destiny or luck (I'd say it's more of the latter), but she finds a man who happens to treat her well and who is in many ways at least trying to be worthy of her.

Patriarchy wants women to believe so many things about men. It wants us to believe that we need men, both to be happy in our everyday lives and to be accepted and respected by society. Along with many other untruths, it wants women to believe that men are scarce so that we are willing to compromise on them.

One of the darkest open secrets that I live with every day is that I both love my life partner and am afraid I love him for the same reason that Jane loves Rochester. He's there, and he pays attention to me. I happen to think with this particular partner I, like Jane, got lucky, and we are well suited in a more urbane way than "hearing voices on the wind." But I happen to believe that, just like Jane, it's only good luck that Peter and I are a good match. I might have chosen him anyway.

Mama and Papa had been married for fifty-nine years when Mama died. And for the last ten years of Mama's life, Papa took better care of her than any nurse has ever taken care of any patient in the history of creation. But before she got sick, he cheated on her so shamelessly, he'd bring his girlfriend around for Shabbat dinners, family birthday parties, and even, most notably in my memory, for my older brother's bar mitzvah photo shoot.

It was just the immediate family: my parents, my brothers and me, and all three of my living grandparents. There should have been eight of us in the room. But there were nine. Papa's girlfriend, Mary, was also there.

Papa called Mary his secretary or his friend. But it was an open secret that they were a couple. I had bought the secretary/friend line until that day in 1993. But Mama and Anyu were not warm to us kids that day, which was out of character. They instead were huddled together, the two of them, whispering. They weren't speaking to Mary and I don't think they were speaking to Papa. Papa was still affectionate and playful. I don't remember, but I bet I hugged and played with him, because he seemed to be the only adult there who was in a good mood. There was a lot of talking going on among the adults, but it was in Hungarian, so I didn't understand. But I suddenly saw Mary with different eyes that day, even as I stood wrapped around the man who had brought her.

Mama threatened to kill herself at least once because of Papa's cheating. She threatened to cheat back at least once as well, flirting openly at a big, fancy event in front of all of their friends. But mostly she just took it. She spent his money and held her nose high and took it. But then, around fifty years into their marriage, when Mama got sick, and Papa happened to be too old to cheat with too many women anyway, I imagine, he was a servant at her feet, a saint.

I think many women have stories like Mama's or mine. Women have, for generations, stood by and had to endure as men did this public-private blend of disrespect. And then children like me have a legacy of watching a man be awful to a woman and not being told, "Look, I am accepting this for complicated reasons. But you should expect more."

Jane didn't even have a couple to look at and respond to an idea of. She had a story, uncorroborated by anyone, that had her uncle lived, he would have been kind to her. But she never saw it. She has literally never in her life been in a relationship with a man who was anything other than entirely abusive to her, like her cousin John and Mr. Brocklehurst. She only knows men as wanting to beat, starve, and humiliate her. And the only counternarrative in her head is one for which she has no real proof. And so Rochester, dream man of all dream men, is alive and he is not brazenly abusive to Jane. He talks to her and takes an interest in her. Of course she falls in love with him. Anyone in her circumstances would.

Women who have been in relationships with men have had a series of secret conversations about men for centuries. We endure certain things, and then, once we admit, in whispers, to a friend what it is we are enduring, we find out that she is putting up with the same thing. We support each other as the disappointments come hitting home for us. Women are just a big group like my grandmothers, who happen to speak the same language and will hold each other by the forearm and give sidelong glances to men who should be ashamed of themselves but are not, and are instead playing with their grandchildren.

Love stories like *Jane Eyre* are part of the problem for many women. So the key is to read and reread the books until we realize that they are secret conversations warning us about good men. *Jane Eyre* is not about falling in love with Rochester. It is about how women need to be willing to break their own hearts in order to dispel the myths that patriarchy wants us to believe, in order to enter into a relationship that is worthy of us.

The men shown to us in love stories like *Jane Eyre* or that of my grandparents are too self-satisfied and too cowardly to break our hearts entirely. It's patriarchy scripting the idea of a psycho woman. They do not want to break up with us because we are good for them. They hurt us, and maybe cause us death by eighteen trillion paper cuts. But patriarchy encourages men to never actually go through the

> *Jane Eyre* is a lesson in how to break one's own heart.

technical heartbreaking themselves. And so *Jane Eyre* is a lesson in how to break one's own heart.

My partner, Peter, and I had been together for five months when it became very clear to me that we could not be together. He never wanted to get married again, or live with anyone again. He didn't want more kids. Then he suddenly started talking a lot about wanting to move back to Europe one day and, come to think of it, sooner rather than later. He would talk openly, in front of me, about a future that I was not in. I didn't make comments about it or discuss it with him. One day, he was dropping me off in the car, and I simply said to him, "This is over. I won't change my mind. You don't want me enough." And I got out of the car. I then gulped for air and sobbed in public.

I had broken my own heart. And it was one of the best things that I ever did. I didn't know what I was doing and I did not calculate this decision. It was a crazed act of an exhausted, hurt person. It was a moment of clarity that I happened to seize upon, rather than letting it pass. But I pulled off a ritual that I think is an important one for women who are enthralled by men who were raised in this ecosystem: the breaking of one's own heart. The expression is, If you love something, set it free. But I think we should change it to, If you love yourself, smash a relationship, just once.

For years before Peter, I was looking for someone, just about anyone. I would break up with people if I realized that I really couldn't stand them, but short of that, I was just on the hunt for female respectability—the right to have strong opinions about diamonds and school districts and the right to be seen as wanted despite my waist size or because of it; God would only ever know. That day in the car with Peter, I decided I wasn't going to cajole or wait. I wasn't going to do what many women I know have done: give ultimatums and cry. I just broke my own heart and got out of the car so I couldn't take it back. And I learned how to do that from Jane.

I picked one prayer from *Jane Eyre* that Stephanie and I had worked on together. It seemed a deeply female prayer, the prayer of the woman who is looking at a man whom she has chosen simply because he is there and paying attention to her. It is a prayer that I believe women have been saying to themselves since the beginning of time:

> I can live alone, if self-respect and circumstances require me so to do. I need not sell my soul to buy bliss. I have an inward treasure born with me, which can keep me alive if all extraneous delights should be withheld.

"I can live alone," it starts. "I can live alone." This phrase admits both strength and vulnerability. It is a clear statement of strength, reminding us that one is strong enough to live alone in this vast, endless world. But it is vulnerable in that it admits that one deeply prefers not to live alone. It is a reminder that we are all one catastrophe away from living alone, and that while that loneliness would be survivable, it would be almost unendurable, for it is not the way we are meant to live. "I can live alone" is a reminder that we are meant to live in communion with something. It is a reminder of why we read, why we gather, why we yearn. We can live alone; we should live in community. But if self-respect and circumstances require it of us, then by God, we can and will live alone.

"I can live alone" is also a reminder that solitude is in fact endurable, and it must be, for it is inevitable. Solitude should be practiced. We will all lose friends and loved ones. We will all retreat into death, which is a lonely path. We should practice for this loneliness and we should remind ourselves of our strength in the face of it by praying, "I can live alone."

Then the prayer continues: "if self-respect and circumstances require me so to do." This phrase is a reminder that we live in a reciprocal relationship with the world. Our character, our personalities, come together with the outside world to make up our fate. Praying this line made me see it as a humble admission that we are not in control of our lives, of whether we will be alone or healthy or poor. We are born into circumstances that can give more breathing room to the possibility of self-respect or create a very limited opportunity for it. Our character determines our fate. World forces determine our fate. "Self-respect and circumstances" prayed as two interconnected concepts remind us of our agency and our helplessness.

"I need not sell my soul to buy bliss." When I pray this line I remember that there will be opportunities to sell my soul—to get quick fixes of something that will feel like bliss. To buy the new shoes I don't need instead of donating the money or saving it to go visit a faraway friend. And when I pray this line I also remember that good things happen without my intervention. Bliss comes all the time without my compromising myself. Praying this line reminds me of hope.

And finally, "I have an inward treasure, born with me, which can keep me alive if all extraneous delights should be withheld." This line, prayed, conjures an image of something divine within me. And it reminds me of that same sacredness in all others, everyone in this room, everyone I can see, everyone I cannot even imagine. This line moves me in its innocence and frustrates me in its lie, as if one's soul or sacredness is enough to keep them alive. It inspires me to help create a world in which it could be true, a world of plenty where one's sacredness would be all one needed.

But this prayer is not uttered by Jane.

Jane is already in love with Rochester when this prayer gets spoken. One night, his bed is set on fire by the awful Grace Poole, and Jane notices the smoke and saves Rochester's life. The two of them have an incredibly intimate moment together, in which Rochester holds Jane's hand and says to her, "You have saved my life. I have a pleasure in owing you so great a debt. . . . Nothing else that has being would have been tolerable to me in the character of creditor for such an obligation: but you: it is different—I feel your benefits no burden, Jane."

And the next day, he is gone. While he is gone, Jane realizes that she is completely in love with him. And then she goes about systematically breaking her own heart. She finds out from Mrs. Fairfax, the housekeeper, that Rochester has gone to visit Miss Ingram, whom he is rumored to have a serious flirtation with. Jane does not write in her diary about how much she loves, misses, and pines for Rochester. She does not confide in her ward's nanny, Sophie, that she is in love with the master of the house. She does not write Rochester a letter of longing. Instead, she forces herself to draw Miss Ingram, as beautifully as she can possibly imagine her, and then draw the plainest, ugliest version of herself that she can. She crushes her own heart. When Rochester returns weeks later, he brings a huge party with him, including the woman, Miss Ingram, whom it is rumored he wants to marry.

One night, when the entire party, including Jane, is gathered in the parlor, waiting for Mr. Rochester to return from an errand, a fortune-telling gypsy arrives at the door of the house. All of the rich people at the party have their fortunes told, but the gypsy won't leave because she says there is one more member of the party who she can sense needs to be seen: Jane. Jane gets led into seeing the gypsy, and the preceding prayer is what the gypsy says that she can see in Jane's face. The gypsy is, of course, Rochester in drag.

It is an incredible ability that Rochester has of reading Jane's face. He is right. Jane can live alone, and will if she needs to. She will jump out of a car, once she realizes that "here" and "paying attention" are not enough. But Rochester is able to see this in her before she has to act on it. Disguised as a woman, Rochester, the most self-indulgent man to ever be written about, is able to see that Jane would be willing to walk away from him if she had to.

Now, in fairness to Peter, this trip where I broke up with him for talking about a future that I was not in was not a normal trip. We were visiting his dying mother. I thought I was seeing a truth in his moment of crisis, not a blip. And I thought it would be cruel of me to be disingenuously by his side for such an important part of his life. So I got out of the car and cracked my heart in half, picturing his beautiful life without me, back in

Europe, unmarried, unmarred, again and again in my head, to convince myself that I was doing the right thing. Not that I was engaging in an act of self-loathing and not that I had broken up with a man I loved and cared for while his mother was dying.

Being heartbroken is a gift. It is an acute pain that passes. And women should break their own hearts at least once, to prove to themselves that they will not settle for "here and paying attention to me."

Peter and I got back together four months later, when I realized that I did not miss *a* man, but this man. He was truly the first man I was willing to walk away from, and the first I wanted to return to. And the willingness to walk away was so important to me. It means that I know that if he ever breaks my heart, I will survive. If he brings his mistress to our grandchild's bar mitzvah, I won't have to simply hold on to my in-law's arm; I will be able to say, "We're done here."

My grandmother, in the last years of her life, could not have lived alone. That is the brutal truth that women have known. Many women, when the moment was right, poisoned their husband's beer or otherwise found a way to get away. But the years of malnutrition caught up with my grandmother when she was in her early seventies, and her back crumbled. She had cement put in, and rods. All for naught. She once held my hand as she collapsed onto the dining room table, putting her head down like a scolded child in the second grade, and smiled at me. I asked if she was okay and she whispered, "No."

Nations collapse and attack us, storms flood us, and bodies break. We need each other. That's why I really think it might be best to break our own hearts, to prove that we can survive anything and then still love the cause of our heartbreak—whether that be a friend, a sibling, a daughter, or a lover. We need community. And we need to remember how strong we are on our own.

We have to be willing to walk away from someone for our own sake. And we have to be willing to go back for the same reason.

CHAPTER EIGHT

On Resentment

She was resolved to consider me bad to the last;
because to believe me good would give her no generous
pleasure: only a sense of mortification.

—Chapter 21, *Jane Eyre*

Whchen Jane leaves Aunt Reed's house in Gateshead to go
to the Lowood Institution at the age of ten, she leaves
Aunt Reed with this declaration:

> I declare I do not love you: I dislike you the worst of
> anybody in the world . . . I am glad you are no rela-
> tion of mine. I will never call you aunt again as long
> as I live. I will never come to visit you when I am
> grown up; and if any one asks me how I liked you, and
> how you treated me, I will say the very thought of you

makes me sick, and that you treated me with miserable cruelty.

Although Jane is a kid when she gives this speech, I am going to defend it. This sermon is a defense of resentment. Resentment is a virtue. And I can prove it.

I have a family member whom I resent deeply. And this person looms overly large in my psyche.

Before I defend resentment, it is important that I tease it out from hate. Hate is often understandable, but is just as often dangerous. To hate is to wish to overpower and annihilate. To hate is an act of aggression. Hate is about the ability to dehumanize the other, reduce them to an object without complexity. There are moments of hatred that are, of course, completely justifiable. Victims often hate their perpetrators. But victims do not serve on the juries of their perpetrators' hearings. And I worry (for myself and all of us who do on occasion hate) that it is like that adage about taking poison and expecting the other person to die. Hate is understandable, but it's often best to be worked through and let go.

Another key difference between resentment and hatred is that hatred can be about any number of things: a wounded ego, a dislike of a person's manners, or just finding someone somehow deeply aesthetically unappealing. Hate is often about race, religion, and fear. All of this is to say that there is easily injustice in hatred. The way white supremacists look at people of color is with hate. It's about a desire to oppress.

Resentment is something else entirely.

Resentment is a controlled fire. It is about feeling a deep sense of unfairness at being treated a certain way, and sitting with that feeling. It is an important feeling. It is a feeling that makes you notice injustice. It is a feeling that helps you articulate what you are witnessing and separate yourself from it. It is a feeling that creates a distance between you and your object, and it is better than hate in that very important way. Hate creates an intimacy with an enemy, an obsession. Resentment creates a protective, almost physical land of armistice.

Resentment in its purest form is rooted in a feeling of having been treated unjustly and is therefore an assertion of your own humanity and your own demands to be treated in the fullness of your humanity. Obviously when we feel we have been treated unfairly, it is not always true. We often feel entitled to things that we demonstrably are not entitled to; hence the joke about white people asking to speak to managers. Or Trump once telling the *New York Times* that they owed him a positive headline. But I think that feeling of indignation at being treated unfairly, that feeling of resentment, is at least a compass that leads to some good, quick, self-therapy-based, "Why do I feel this way?" questions. And we have to demand fairness, if not out loud, then in our own private, righteous indignation.

If we allow ourselves to be treated unfairly, we will stand for more and more unfairness in the world. We have to stay attuned to our resentment so that our antennae are sharpened when we see unfairness out in the world and think: *Wait! I feel resentment coming! Something might actually be unfair!* Emotions help us notice that something is going on around us, so that we can try to change the thing on the outside the way pain teaches us to stop running into that corner of the coffee table.

You can diagnose someone as unhealthy for you or figure out that they are toxic and abusive and therefore remove yourself from them without hating them. Hating them does not help you behave more healthily any faster. Hate is an "activation" emotion only in destructive ways; it does not motivate you to notice things about yourself and then make good choices. Hate might rise up within us, but I think we should kiss it on the cheek and send it on its way as quickly as we can manage.

I have, of course, said the words "I hate them" about many people. And I am sure that, at least for passing moments, I have actually felt that way. With my relative, though, it's not hatred. I can describe the resentment for you; it's simple. I don't wish them harm in a general way. I don't want them to get into a car accident or to get a cancer diagnosis. Those two things feel extreme, and I worry that they would learn the wrong lessons from them. With the cancer or car accident scenario they could tell a story of being angelic in some way, a beautiful victim.

I want them to be humbled in exactly the ways that they have been awful to me and my family. I want their punishment to be a lesson catered to my diagnosis of their awfulness. I want a Greek punishment. I want the gods to send back the two dogs of mine that they promised they would take care of but instead lost, and have them bark from ten p.m. to two a.m. each night. That's how I resent them; I am indignant that the world allows them to walk around unpunished, and so I want them to learn and be haunted by their own mistakes. I don't want to punish them myself; I want the world to right itself and teach them. Resentment is a feeling about the world that we pin on something smaller. We resent the medical system, so we get mad at the nurse. We resent how the corporation takes insidious shortcuts in the name of serving their shareholders, which has led to the interminable length of time we've been sitting on hold to cancel a service we never signed up for—so we are rude to the customer service representative. Resentment is important, but it must be controlled. It must be used with intention, lest we simply continue its cycle by sending home a customer service representative who is then resentful of their rude clients.

Resenting this person has, most important, allowed me to cut them out of my life, to say to my imaginary version of them, "You are unhealthy for me. I am scared of you." (I am too scared to say this to their face.) Resenting them has forced me to make sure that I stay away from people who remind me of them, or maybe, more specifically, whose behavior makes me feel a certain way that reminds me of the way my relative's behavior makes me feel.

The complication of resentment comes with empathy. If we resent someone rather than hate them, we will be in conversation with empathy. Questions come into my mind like: Can I imagine a possibility in which they are not a bad person but a misunderstood person, who I should not be in touch with, but who I do not resent or wish for dogs to bark at them in perpetuity? I often have thought about empathizing with this person and then shied away from it. But what is at risk for me if I never empathize with them? Will they haunt me?

I, of course, want to believe in empathy and do in many circumstances, especially when I am invited by a specific person to empathize with them. Virginia Woolf said that war is a lack of imagination—that we would never be able to shoot each other if we were able to imagine the interiority of one another. And I absolutely think that is true. I believe in serious consideration of prison abolition because locking someone up indicates a similar lack of imagination.

What I can do for this relative is what Woolf asks me to do: imagine. I can write stories about this person that make their behavior understandable. I can imagine things that are possible. I can imagine abuses that they very well could have endured. I can imagine the way they perceive things, the stories they tell themselves. But at the end of the day, I don't know if any of what I imagine about this person is true. So by empathizing in a vacuum, the very vacuum I need to be in for my own safety, what I am doing is erasing them.

Jane's relationship with Aunt Reed is obviously more dire than my relationship with my relative. Aunt Reed abused Jane and then sent her away to be starved and to all but die at the Lowood Institution.

After Jane has made Thornfield her home, and while Miss Ingram is still there visiting and seemingly trying to seduce Mr. Rochester, Jane gets a summons back to Gateshead—back to the woman whom she would never call aunt again.

Jane finds out that her cousin John, the boy who used to torture her, is dead after squandering almost all of the Reeds' fortune on gambling, drinking, and women. Mrs. Reed denied John's last request for money and now he is dead, which is literally killing his mother. A Greek punishment is given to Mrs. Reed.

Jane immediately agrees to go to her aunt. There is no hesitation. There is no moment of fear, of wondering if her aunt is just going to humiliate and be awful to her yet again. Jane is granted time off by Mr. Rochester and is off to visit her former abuser as quickly as possible.

She then has to travel considerably in order to grant this request of Mrs. Reed's. Mrs. Reed does not give a sign of having been changed or humbled in the way that she gives her request. There is no supplication, no "I know that this is a lot to ask." She is behaving, even in this request, as entitled as ever, clearly unaware of and uncaring about the difficulties that she is causing for Jane, who has to put her livelihood at risk, spend much money, and leave Rochester to flirt without her watchful eye in order to go to the woman whom she formerly called aunt.

I wonder if there were different circumstances under which Jane would not have gone. If it were merely a summons, without the pathetic circumstances outlined, I wonder if Jane would have gone with such quick, decisive conviction and seemingly so little thought and worry for herself. But these are the circumstances that Jane is given, and all we know is that she goes.

When Jane finally gets into the sickroom to see Mrs. Reed, it is not a sweet apology or tearful regrets that meet her. Reconciliation is in no way being offered. In fact, it is a version of the very worst possibility that meets Jane inside that room.

Jane has made clear that she wishes to be reconciled with her aunt, to use this opportunity of a deathbed to come to a sort of peace with her past and her family. Jane wishes to forget and forgive all that happened between her and her aunt. When she walks into Aunt Reed's sickroom she says, "How are you, dear aunt?" She has not forgotten the promise she made as a child. She reminds us that "I had once vowed that I would never call her aunt again." Jane then takes Aunt Reed's hand and confesses to us how much it would mean to her if Aunt Reed pressed her hand in return. But Aunt Reed does not; instead, she turns her head and pointedly takes her hand away.

Aunt Reed at least partially validates the extent of Jane's hurt by saying that Jane was "born to be [her] torment." I think I would take great delight in hearing that from the relative whom I resent.

Aunt Reed then confesses that she has committed a sin against Jane that Jane does not know about. She has Jane pull out a letter from another uncle, offering to adopt and take care of her. Aunt Reed now confesses that she responded to the letter three years ago, replying that Jane Eyre was dead. When Jane asks why she would do that, Aunt Reed responds that she could not stand the idea that Jane would be comfortable and loved. Jane immediately tells her aunt to forget it and offers her love and comfort, which Aunt Reed again rebuffs.

What we see happen between Aunt Reed and Jane is what I would most fear—that trusting my relative again would prove to be a mistake. That I could take something like being invited to their deathbed the wrong way, and they would sting me like a viper again. And while I of course do not judge Jane in this chapter, but rather feel lacking compared with her pious example, I know that I would not thrive in her shoes. I'd feel smacked. And my biggest fear with my relative is that I could keep rising higher, be more and more forgiving, and all I would be given back is more and more pain.

But maybe my resentment keeps them safe too. There was a German philosopher who is now Saint Teresa Benedicta of the Cross but was born Edith Stein. She was born Jewish and by way of atheism became a Catholic—not just a Catholic but a Carmelite nun. Stein felt that empathy was an act of imagining through which we can figure out others' spiritual realities and our own. She says empathy is an experience of another person's experience. Empathy is a prerequisite for knowledge of others and of the self.

Here is the flip side of Woolf's call for empathy as an anti-war strategy. It works as an argument against hate. It works to keep us from dehumanizing one another entirely. But imagination also invents the other. In order to empathize well, you have to listen. And I cannot listen to this person. They are bad for me.

Which is why, when I consider Woolf's idea of imagining things about this relative, I come up short in such intimate relationships (though I love it as an anti-war strategy). I am afraid that I will have played a trick on myself, one that will dismiss my resentment enough that I will make a bad decision. If I tell myself stories of miscommunication, their own abuse, their good intentions, then I run the risk of going to them, only to have it made clear to me that they were even worse than I had feared all along. My resentment keeps me safe.

Woolf was right that imagination is an important anti-war and anti-hate effort. But she also loved gossip and petty resentments and would revel in them as if worming her way into an old, comfortable couch. We should use imagination and empathy to keep us out of war, but we should use resentment to keep us from over-empathizing and therefore erasing people who are right there, being entirely themselves and hurting us. We have to listen to empathize. And while we maybe should listen to the people whom we hate in order to re-humanize them, we shouldn't force ourselves to listen to those we may resent for good reason.

Jane says about her aunt that "she was resolved to consider me bad to the last; because to believe good would give her no generous pleasure; only a sense of mortification." And on this, Jane and I agree. My relative would be horrified by any attempt of generosity on my part. In fact, I think they would love this sermon; I think they'd be delighted that they can finally feel a sense of validation of my contempt, which I have never made entirely clear to them. I won't name them and give them the satisfaction; a lovely side effect of my unwillingness to do so is that multiple people might see themselves in this chapter.

Resentment can save empathy from itself. The danger of hate is that you make the other inhuman, which deprives you of some of your own humanity. A resentful empathy means you recognize the other as human and subject to circumstances and instincts and hurts, but your resentment disallows you from getting too specific and projecting too much: "I still just don't understand how they could have done this." And that's the only place from which to judge, right? Hate judges too harshly. Excess empathy judges not at all, which is its own form of disrespect.

Jane, in this scene, both pushes me in my attachment to resentment and validates my attachment to a certain version of it. On the one hand Jane gets what I want as far as Greek punishment of a tormentor goes, and it does nothing for her. She is not pleased or relieved that Aunt Reed has been given her just deserts. And I think that is important for me to know. I wouldn't actually take joy in watching this person suffer. My resentment does keep me from Jane's additional hurt. But in a final turn, Jane finds out she has an uncle, ready to love her, because she risked putting her resentment aside long enough to go to her aunt when she was beckoned. Maybe that is what I need to learn from Jane. If this person reaches out to me, I can find a way to respond without resentment. But until then, I can hold on to my resentment to keep me safe and them entirely human.

This is Stein's paradox of empathy. Identifying with a person is what makes you understand their suffering, but it can also risk embellishing their unique suffering with your imagination. The person who cries while they grieve with you is really just making your grief about them. That is not a helpful empathy; that is annoying.

CHAPTER NINE

On Women's Anger

It was a savage face . . . it removed my veil from
its gaunt head, rent it in two parts, and flinging
both on the floor, trampled on them.

—Chapter 25, *Jane Eyre*

Jane comes back to Thornfield after burying Aunt Reed. She
has been gone much longer than she had planned, and so
much more has happened back at Thornfield than she had
imagined would in her absence.

Almost immediately upon her return, she hears from Mrs.
Fairfax, Thornfield's housekeeper, that Rochester has all but
proposed to Miss Ingram. The preplanning phase of the wedding appears to be in great motion. Jane is crushed by these
updates, but she lifts her chin and goes to Rochester to quit.
She tells him that Adele should be sent to boarding school and

that she, Jane, must find a new situation. Instead of agreeing with her (or after agreeing with her in order to see her response and be completely sure that she is in love with him), he proposes.

She needs some convincing, not because she doesn't love him and want to marry him but because she does not believe that he really wants to marry her. In fact, she thinks that he is mocking her with the proposal. But he manages, through one of the most romantic scenes in all the books that I have read (and I love romantic books), to convince her that he really wants her, loves her, chooses her. He asks her to do all sorts of romantic things, like "give me my name" and "walk through this earth by my side." The best is when he asks her to be his "best earthly companion," a phrase I have read and reread so many times, it is burnt onto my retinas.

They set a date for a wedding as quickly as they can arrange it. He insists on the short engagement and she, in turn, insists that they maintain some distance during that short month, to test his commitment and her self-restraint. He takes her shopping, in a scene in which we find out that Adele has a better understanding of Jane's tastes than Rochester does, because Rochester simply wants to shower Jane with everything he can give her. Jane and Rochester have a tour of Europe planned; they are to take off straight from the wedding. He's bought a new, shiny coach for them to ride far away from Thornfield in style.

Jane turns down almost all of Rochester's proffered gifts. She instead takes simple fabric from him, to make dignified gowns befitting a version of her soon-to-be station. She refuses to wear the Rochester family's jewelry, saying that she would look ridiculous covered in diamonds. She keeps him at arm's length, not trusting this gift of a happy life unfolding in front of her, wanting to make sure that her behavior stays beyond reproach.

Rochester is frustrated by the way Jane is keeping him at a distance. She won't spend much time one-on-one with him. She won't kiss or embrace him. He is frustrated that she will not let him dress her like a queen or prepare a proper trousseau for her, which would be completely appropriate under the circumstances. So he finds a loophole on the last point. She requires a veil for the wedding, so he buys her the most expensive, elaborate veil that he can find. When she sees the gift in her room, she unpacks it. Rochester is off settling some business before the wedding and their long honeymoon. She privately laughs at him and prepares to tease him for insisting on dressing her up as someone she isn't. She packs the veil back into its box. Rochester is not back from his errands; she will have to tease him the following day.

But that night, two nights before the wedding, Jane has a

vision, a vivid dream that interrupts her plans of teasing Rochester. While she is lying in bed, unsure whether she is asleep, she sees a figure in her room that deeply startles her, as much as the moment in the red room. When Rochester is back, the night before their wedding, she tells him about the vision and how terrifying it was. The vision was of a woman Jane had never seen before. During the vision/dream, the woman goes into Jane's closet, takes out the veil, and puts it on her own head. Jane doesn't see the woman's face for a long time, just her vague form in some kind of white garment.

Jane sees the woman's face only when the woman steps in front of the mirror to look at herself in Jane's veil—and an awful description is given of this face. Jane says that she wishes she could forget the "discolored," "savage" face that was "blackened." She tells Rochester that a "savage face[d]" creature put the veil on. Then it "removed [it] from its gaunt head, rent it in two parts, and flinging both on the floor, trampled on them."

As we will explore more in later chapters, we find out on the day of the wedding that this "vampire" is not actually a bloodsucking monster but instead is Rochester's wife, Bertha. We further find out that Bertha has been locked in the attic for ten years, from the time when Rochester deemed her insane and unbearable for him to live with as her husband.

Rochester's attempt to keep Bertha a secret, locked up and

causing as little trouble to him as possible, while assuaging his conscience seems to be an unsuccessful endeavor, a futile attempt of the truly privileged. Bertha's well-paid guard, Grace Poole, has a drinking problem. And Bertha is smart (the book's word is "cunning"), so sometimes she is able to steal a key and break out of her room when Grace passes out from too much gin.

Bertha seems to mostly haunt the house at night, when she is able to break out of her domestic trap. But we only definitively hear of her romping around the house on two occasions. And on both of these, she commits acts of deep rage.

One of these acts, the one toward the man who locked her up, is also violent. She lights Rochester's bed on fire while he is asleep in it. The second is this one, in which in she rips Jane's wedding veil two nights before the wedding.

The ripping of the veil is a different kind of violence than lighting the bed on fire. The veil was a gift from Rochester. She probably recognizes his taste (we know that his taste is triumphant) and that it is a bridal veil. She rips it but does not hurt Jane. She rips it, stomps on it, and leaves the room. She leaves Jane still safely tucked into her bed, although of course we know that Bertha could have easily, at minimum, lit the bed on fire.

Bertha's ability to act so differently in these two situations— when she finds Rochester in bed and when she finds Jane in bed—to me demonstrates that she is not a woman who is completely mentally incapacitated or out to destroy everything in front of her. She could kill Grace Poole whenever Grace is passed out, and does not. But when her brother comes to visit her, she stabs him.

> Bertha is not a madwoman; she is an angry woman.

Bertha is not a madwoman. A madwoman would not be able to control her rage, whereas Bertha is in complete control; she directs her rage at the man who locks her up and the brother who lets her be locked up, not the woman who is paid to take care of her, or the other woman who will, from Bertha's perspective, be his next victim. Bertha is not a madwoman; she is an angry woman.

Patriarchy likes to confuse these two things, but rage and mental illness, while sometimes related, are hugely different. And rage and madness, while they are not the same, can of course be interconnected.

Obviously, many of us are not locked up in attics or anything near. But there are millions and millions of women who are locked up in proverbial attics—who are in abusive relationships, trapped taking care of a loved one in a way that feels unrewarding and undervalued, not allowed to seek careers, and any number of other versions of being locked up entirely. But even for those of us who are as free as women get—women like me who make their own living, are highly educated, and are as free as one can imagine being in this systematically flawed world—there are times when we are put into situations in which we have only two choices: to be a bitch or to be someone's bitch.

These are almost always situations in which someone else is (either mindlessly or intentionally) using the woman to his own ends rather than treating her as a human being with an independent will, agenda, and sense of self. This is the version of the woman whose ideas are stolen right in front of her in the boardroom, who is told to stop being a pain in the ass when she asks a question, or is asked to hold a beer even when flat surfaces abound. I mean, what are you standing on, Rochesters?

Of course it is convenient for patriarchy to diminish our mental capacity when we start demanding things and when we are raving at injustice. But most of the time, really, we are just angry. We just want to not be interrupted, not locked up. We want to be appreciated for our work and allowed to play our sports in peace.

Sometimes we really do start to behave in a way that appears unhinged from "appropriate" behavior. Years of having to guard a woman in an attic drives us to drinking gin. We get really mad when all you did was ask us to hold a beer. You gaslight us by telling us that you were just joking, when we both know that you were being lewd. You piss us off and drive us crazy and then get mad at us for being either of those things—mad that we don't want you to dress us up as dolls, and so you buy us veils.

I have found myself in these situations too many times in my life, and yet fewer than many women. These were situations in which I felt as though my only two options were to let myself be steamrolled or to call someone out (usually publicly).

I remember lots of smaller incidents in which I felt trapped. I am trained as a chaplain. I am supposed to live a life of kindness, compassion, and empathy. But I always try to choose being a bitch over being someone's bitch. And I said *choose*. It's a conscious choice. I pause. I think about it. I breathe. And if I am capable of it, then I choose being a bitch.

I am called confrontational, a pain in the ass, and worse—often enough that I wonder if on some level I enjoy confrontation and being worse. I have thought a lot about this and considered it because I would hate to think that I simply confront people for the thrill of it. After much thought, I have come to the self-satisfied conclusion that I actually find confrontation scary and uncomfortable. But I find it necessary and a little bit sexy. I cannot stand for someone else to define, even for a moment, who I am to suit his needs—unless, of course, I am scared. I would not let someone do that to someone else in front of me and so I cannot let it happen to me.

I wish that I had the strength to light beds on fire. It feels as though I only really get around to lighting candles to better see my own way.

One of the odd things to me is that when I am called angry or crazy or rageful I am not feeling any of those things. What I am actually feeling, like Bertha, is trapped. I sobbed, unable to catch my breath, after my boss picked me up by the shoulders and shook me. I wasn't mad. I felt like there wasn't anything for me to do. I felt confused. And I felt like I had no recourse. I had just been assaulted and publicly humiliated and there was nothing I could do. I responded in a way that was described as "unprofessional and hysterical." I felt like trash. I felt small and invisible. My body responded without my permission. If I could have gone about my day, that is what I would have chosen to do. But instead, I was so loud. My sobs echoed in the bathroom so loudly that I was sent home, to stop causing a scene. I was a twenty-five-year-old kid who had been shaken by a fifty-year-old chief officer, and I was told to stop embarrassing everyone and go home. My cries were too loud. Too angry. Too mad.

Bertha's anger is magical because it seems to me that she is in

Bertha plays her anger like an orchestra.

complete control of it. My anger comes when I lose control. Bertha plays her anger like an orchestra. She doesn't take out her anger on Jane; she chooses sisterhood, warning another potential victim of Rochester. She takes out her silence, which has festered into rage, on the man who has gagged her and locked her up.

Jane has a whole six-hundred-page novel about her. We learn of her childhood, her education, her employment. We learn about her family and friends. We are inside her head, as she is the one telling the story, and the story she is telling us is one of nuance and complexity.

Bertha's plot points in the novel are simple. As soon as Jane moves to Thornfield Hall to act as a governess, it is clear that something is not right in the mansion. It is only when Bertha is in the way of Jane and Rochester's marriage that the noise-maker in the attic, the fire starter and guest-stabber, the manic laugher and veil render, is given her name. Bertha is the woman who gets in the way of Jane's marriage to Rochester and who then dies so that Jane and Rochester can have their happily ever after. Bertha is the epitome of an instrumentalized woman. She is married for her money and then disposed of when Rochester has the money and no longer enjoys her company. She is sold off by her father. She is exploited by Grace Poole so that Grace can serve her addiction, which is probably fueled by having to guard Bertha. Bertha is treated as a human by no one. She is the example of how patriarchy loves to fetishize women: disposable, serviceable as long as they are fuckable, best to be made invisible as soon as they are not fuckable, and crazy if they choose to make too much noise.

Bertha is complicated and is famous and infamous for both her actions and her described qualities. So when I sat down to embark on this experiment of treating *Jane Eyre* as sacred, I knew that Bertha would give me problems. I am someone who has all but left traditional religion in large part because I do not find that it appropriately accounts for people's suffering. So I was nervous that my favorite novel would come up short in the same way religion does when I got around to Bertha. She, I feared, would not have a theological justification strong enough to satisfy me and my concerns when it comes to the big question of why we let so much suffering happen on our watch.

Bertha and I have gotten close in my time of treating *Jane Eyre* as sacred. She has meant many things to me at different moments. But at this moment, in the midst of a movement, Bertha is the unheard women yet to be accounted for. She is our warning—our caution—and our yet-to-be-dealt-with responsibility. Bertha is the woman who is still unable to speak to even worse crimes being perpetrated against her, even in this revolution.

When her efforts to be free or to wreak havoc upon the men who hold her captive get stifled again and again, she burns the house down several months later. When Rochester tries to save her, she jumps to her death and he gets injured in the flames.

Jane does something very brave and bold once she finds out that Rochester is married and that it isn't Grace causing problems in the attic after all. Rochester offers to take care of Jane financially and have her act as his mistress. He says they can go to France and no one will know that they are not married—a basic NDA that we believe would assure her financial stability and happiness. She, of course, would have no guarantee from him, no legal protections. But in theory, it sounds like a good offer; at minimum there is a promise of comfort and it is very romantic.

Jane instead decides to leave on her own, in the middle of the night, with almost no money. She does not want Rochester to be able to find her, so she changes her name. She struggles terribly for several days, nearly dying from dehydration, exposure, and a broken heart. Her life's plans are thrown away entirely because of Rochester's actions, and she is vulnerable in a way that she hadn't been even as an abandoned orphan.

But she gets taken in by a minister who recognizes her "good breeding" and keeps her warm and safe. Jane gets back on her feet. Then she finds out that she is rich. Then, rich, she finds out her love is available now, and she gets the man.

Bertha gets a head "bashed on cobblestone." Bertha isn't the secret in the attic of *Jane Eyre*. Bertha is the truth at the heart of *Jane Eyre*. Bertha is the silent woman who is seen only when a woman with more power comes forward, but whose options are still nearly impossibly few.

There are a thousand questions that we are asking in the middle of this revolution, and many we could ask about the actions of Jane and Rochester. The questions for right now are: How do we make things right by the victims who have come forward, and what do we do about the women who are still trapped?

We are shown a truly marginalized woman in Bertha, who has been taken advantage of and treated horribly in every way. And her only path to freedom is suicide. Those who are oppressed and have no way out cannot be forced to self-sacrifice to try to get equality. In fact, a forced self-sacrifice is not a self-sacrifice. She can either jump, burn down with the house, or not set the fire and stayed locked up forever. There is no sufficient way for Bertha to combat her situation, so thorough is her abuse.

Jane Eyre, like all sacred things, does not sufficiently account for the suffering of the most marginalized and most vulnerable among us. But maybe it is not up to the things that we treat as sacred to do that work, but up to us to try to do it. Or maybe that is the purpose of sacred texts: to be insufficient and leave us to do our work in the real world.

It is now my pleasure to burn my false idols. And that's when I realized I'm not Jane. I'm Bertha. And I want to bring the whole house tumbling down with me. God's full power will be manifest only in the afterworld or the end-time; that is when divine justice shall be meted out fully—then I will live righteously and hope to meet you in the end-time. And until then, fuck off.

We choke on the bile of our silence and it turns to rage.

Jane does not really get mad in the novel. She does as a child, at Aunt Reed. But by later in the book, she is forgiving, understanding, all the things I am supposed to be, that women are supposed to be in order to be heard. There is a theory that Bertha is a version of Jane, the part of her that was locked in that red room all those years ago. In that way, *Jane Eyre* is *Fight Club* long before *Fight Club*. It is potentially a psychological thriller about how women have to cut themselves in half in order to let out their rage. I love that reading of the novel, but it is not my favorite. My favorite reading is the one in which Rochester falls out of enchantment with Bertha when he meets her mother for the first time and suddenly realizes that Bertha is at least part Black. We now understand through epigenetics that trauma can initiate a gene into action, especially when it comes to mental health. So imagine the trauma of marrying a man you barely know. He marries you for your money. He then enjoys your body for a few months. He then begins to get bored of you. Then he finds out that your mother looks Black and all but disowns you—an argument for intersectional feminism if I ever heard one.

He kidnaps you. He takes you to England—so different from where you grew up in the West Indies. Would you not, maybe, have a psychotic break?

I do not blame Rochester. Nor do I blame individual men for a lot of the actions that some of them engage in. At the time of *Jane Eyre*, a man had all the wealth, ownership, voting rights—everything. Women had nothing. Men were trained to feel not only entitled to women's bodies but responsible for them.

I love a lot about Bertha and her anger. I love that she tries to light Mr. Rochester on fire. I love that she attacks her brother when he comes to visit her. I love that she never tries to attack Grace Poole, or Jane, or Adele, who is the bastard child of one of her husband's affairs that he had while Bertha was locked up in an attic in freezing, rainy, rural England.

Jean Rhys imagined Bertha's point of view in her seminal novel *Wide Sargasso Sea*. In the novel, Rhys goes far outside the bounds of what is discussed in the book, but one does not need to go off the page to have our hearts break for Bertha. The mere idea of being put on a ship and taken four thousand miles away just to be locked up in an attic is enough to make me sick.

I do not believe in violence. I think it is sometimes necessary, but much more infrequently than it is used. So I do not suggest that we use Bertha's strategy for addressing our anger. However, I think there is much that we can learn from the way Bertha expresses her rage. She looks at herself in the mirror; she rips the products of patriarchy; she is loud and persistent. Our anger has been made quiet for too long. We are choking on its flames and being made mad by our sewn lips. It's time to breathe fire and leave behind scorched earth.

CHAPTER TEN

On Love

**I could bend her with my finger and thumb: and what
good would it do?**

—Chapter 27, *Jane Eyre*

When Jane learns that Rochester is married, she has to figure out what it means for her. Even if we don't have experience with finding out that the person we love is married, this type of thing has happened to a lot of us—the person we love isn't who we thought they were and then we have to decide whether we still love them and what to do with this new information.

Rochester's wife, whom Jane had no idea about, lives in the attic right above where Jane lays her head at night, a fact that must haunt Jane for being so obvious and her not seeing it. I'll discuss the wife, Bertha, on her own terms, in more detail later. But before I get to that, I want to consider what the fact of Bertha means for Jane.

In my favorite scene that I have ever read, Rochester tries to convince Jane to stay with him even though she now knows that he is married. It is mere hours after their wedding has been interrupted by Bertha's brother showing up at the altar and having a lawyer claim on Bertha's behalf that Rochester cannot get married because he has a wife and she lives. Everything is raw and right at the surface of Rochester's and Jane's skin and the tips of their tongues. The emotions are ready to boil over, and these two people who love each other spend the entire scene figuring out what this love means for them now that the truth of the attic is out on the lower floors of the house.

We've all heard the expression "Love is not enough." What people mean is that loving someone does not mean you should be in a relationship with them. But I think this scene demonstrates that love, if done right—if you treat the object of your affection with dignity and act with good intentions—is enough.

> Love, if done right, is enough.

It may not mean you should be married. But it is enough.

After the wedding is unceremoniously interrupted, Rochester takes the entire wedding party, which now includes a lawyer and his brother-in-law, up to the attic where he has his wife, Bertha. She is a prisoner and a patient. It is at this moment that Jane learns who has been making so much noise all these months: Bertha. A truth has been violently pacing right above her head that Jane simply hasn't been able to see.

Bertha is described as an animal, as purple, as lunging and spitting, as large and violent. She is said to almost walk on all fours and to be "so cunning; it is not in mortal discretion to fathom her craft." A witch.

Jane watches as Bertha lunges at Rochester and continues to watch Rochester explain who Bertha is and what her temperament is. Jane, through all of it, says nothing. Standing in her wedding gown, she goes to her room and locks herself in, staying silent. She changes into her plain, simple clothes from before her engagement. She silently weeps, alone in her room almost all day.

While sitting in her room she realizes that there is only one thing she can do, only one path forward. She has to leave Thornfield Hall and leave behind the man she loves. It feels inconceivable to her to be torn from this man she worships. But she realizes it is the only thing that she can do. She has been put into such an impossible situation, there are only impossible answers. After she has locked herself up all day, she finally leaves her room for something to eat and drink. Rochester is waiting for her, right outside her door. She faints from hunger and fatigue, and he catches her. He takes care of her and insists that they talk.

Rochester, for all his faults (and they are many), knows Jane and truly loves her. But despite his deep understanding of her, he cannot fathom that she might leave him. When she says that she is indeed leaving, we watch him push away the idea as preposterous. He cannot imagine his life without her, and his response reads like the denial of someone who has just found out about the death of a loved one. When a friend of mine died in a car accident I remember saying, "She's not dead. I just saw her yesterday," as if a day could not be enough time for someone to do something as big as die. Rochester is in a similar frame of mind in this scene. Just this morning they were to be married. Just this morning his life's happiness was secured. It is not possible that, mere hours later, he and Jane are going to be parted forever. There hasn't been enough time for something so big to happen, for his life to be so thoroughly thwarted in a mere day.

As she talks about how she must leave him, and as it begins to sink in, at least in part, the idea makes him desperate, a lion freshly caught and locked in a cage of a new, brutal reality. But Jane has accidentally gotten locked in the cage with him. His happiness is bound up in being with her. He has been searching for years for his "best earthly companion" and has found it in

Jane's small frame. The idea of it being taken from him now is not one he is willing to entertain, at least not peacefully. He does what any of us would do if someone were taking away the dearest thing in the world to us. He tries everything he can think of to try to keep her with him.

He tells her his story of woe. It works; she pities him. But it does not work enough to get her to stay. He tries appealing to her goodness. It works; she forgives him. But again, it does not work well enough to get her to stay. He tries to bribe her; he promises to take her to the French Riviera, where no one will know they aren't married. She sees the logic in this offer, but again she says no. He tries being cruel, reminding her of her profound aloneness in the world by saying, "Is it better to drive a fellow-creature to despair than to transgress a mere human law—no man being injured by the breach? For you have neither relatives nor acquaintances whom you need fear to offend." It works again; she agrees. But still, she stays resolved to be parted from him.

She wants to go with him. But she says, "Laws and principles are not for the times when there is no temptation: they are for such moments as this, when body and soul rise in mutiny against their rigor; stringent are they; inviolate they shall be." Her body and soul want to stay with Rochester. But she pronounces that she must respect herself and leave him.

If Jane Eyre had a superpower, it would be her incredible ability to taxonomize herself. She has said to Rochester in the past: "I am not talking to you now through the medium of custom, conventionalities, nor even of mortal flesh:—it is my spirit that addresses your spirit." Later she says, "My spirit is willing to do what is right; and my flesh, I hope, is strong enough to accomplish the will of Heaven." And in this scene, when Rochester is begging her to stay with him, she tells us that "while he spoke my very conscience and reason turned traitors against me, and charged me with crime in resisting him. They spoke almost as loud as Feeling." Conscience, reason, and feeling are discernibly different to Jane. She can hear each of their voices separately, rather than only hearing them in an indecipherable harmony.

She can do what many of us only wish we could. She can compartmentalize herself—hear that her heart is saying one thing while her mind says another and her thumbnail says another, weigh all the voices, and make a conclusion as to whom she should listen to. She treats her emotions like a panel of doctors whose opinions she values, but at the end of the day, she chooses the expert with the relevant specialty to address the corresponding condition.

Rochester has a similar knack, but only when it comes to Jane. He cannot separate himself into bits, but he can see all the parts of her in addition to being able to see their great sum.

In fact, he says that there is a physical cord of communion between the two of them, "somewhere under my left ribs." He says it is "tightly and inextricably knotted to a similar string situated in the corresponding quarter of [Jane's] little frame."

Rochester does not tell us that he knows it, but he loves in large part with his eyes. He watches Jane and watches out for her. He is her best observer. He knows her and understands her. He wishes better for her than she wishes for herself. His knowing her materially matters to his ability to love her. And his ability to see her body in all its parts determines how he will handle this crucial moment in their relationship.

The apex of the conversation finally comes around. He has yelled. She has wept. They have fought, pleaded, begged, and prayed. They are in that moment of a fight in which you are both still in the room because you don't want to be far away from your beloved, but the truth is, everything that can be said has been said.

It is then that it occurs to Rochester that he has one act of recourse that he hasn't considered: he could rape her. He could rape her and then she would either get pregnant or not but it would definitely change the situation. She would have to think of herself differently if he raped her.

What he says is, "I could bend her with my finger and thumb: and what good would it do . . . Conqueror I might be of the house, but the inmate would escape to heaven before I could call myself possessor of its clay dwelling-place. . . . it is you, spirit, that I want."

I don't believe in spirits. But I think the word *spirit* is a great approximation of an idea that few other words try to encapsulate. There is something interior about each human that makes them as unique as a fingerprint. We can hide this thing about ourselves, and it is not something that can be seen by others without permission. This thing—this "soul"—can be broken without permission; Rochester would risk breaking it by raping Jane. But it cannot be seen without permission. This soul is the thing that some women in basements manage to keep alive and well despite their surroundings and the crimes against them. It is the thing that we should try to cherish in each other and create space for each of ours to shine. Rochester is contemplating breaking it in order to keep the house it lives in—and decides not to. I love this about him.

I know how this sounds. I know what you must be thinking: "Wow, Vanessa. He *doesn't* rape her! What a mensch! Shouldn't we want more from our men than 'not rapists'?" And yes. Of course it's not enough. (Although I would say that a man who truly, deeply understands and respects consent is actually quite a rare and radical thing.) But I think Rochester is saying more than "I won't rape you."

What Rochester is doing is thinking out loud. This is a man who prides himself on a lack of cruelty. It is a time in which he could beat his wife legally and have her sent away to a lunatic asylum and be the one to get sympathy. This is a time when white male privilege wasn't a system of rewards that happened to be by-products of laws but was explicitly law. And he is saying, There is something I could do that would ensure that I get what I want. But he chooses, with all his laws, money, and stature, not to be the conqueror. I don't even think what he really wants is to possess her spirit so much as he wants her to willingly show it to him. He knows that if he attacks her she will never reveal the secrets within her.

On the simplest, grossest level of oversimplification, men have power because they are usually bigger. That's it. That's the whole reason for pay gaps and genital mutilation and girls in basements and the rest of it. And Rochester, in this moment, remembers that essential fact. He remembers that he is bigger and performs a taxonomy on his own body, a trick he has learned from Jane, and chooses to leave his body at the side.

Whenever men use their size as a weapon near me, I get so bored. I am sure that this boredom is a defense mechanism. I cannot control what they will do with their larger bodies; being afraid does nothing. I find their strutting obvious and deeply, deeply dull. It is dull because it's so obvious and also because anything that doesn't make me think is boring. And a man who is flexing his size is putting me in a position in which my thoughts are useless. His size is all that matters.

Rochester is saying that Jane's size and her body are both irrelevant, but he is saying that his body is irrelevant too. He only wants the interesting parts of her and only wants to offer the interesting parts of himself to her. And he says all of that while in the midst of the most desperate moment of his life.

I love this scene because Rochester does something that I don't think I would be capable of. He sees a chess move he could make to take the queen captive, and he leaves the move on the board. I truly believe that if someone was taking everything that mattered away from me, I would do everything I could to keep it, even things that destroyed it. I am deeply worried that I wouldn't just cut off my own nose to spite my face but to save my nose. I talk all the time about how I will put my dog down before she is in too much pain. I chant it to anyone who will listen. I basically make it sound like I want to kill her while she is still young and healthy, like any day I'm ready to call in a vet and euthanize her while she eats peanut butter, just for fun. I recite this plan in order to train myself and psych myself up for the time when I will actually have to pull out a whole jar of Jif (what I project to be her favorite) and call the vet to come over. Because I know how far I will go out of my way to avoid moments of desperation. I guess what I'm saying is that I am worried that if I were Rochester, I would rape Jane. And so I admire him for not raping her. And I think the thing that saves Rochester in this moment is a really wonderful, strong version of love.

The feeling of love seems so close to the feeling of wanting to consume something. My stepdaughters, who are not of my own flesh, are sometimes so overwhelmingly dear to me that I want to eat their cheeks. The instinct of love is just that; it is an instinct toward intimacy. To love someone is to yearn to know and cherish every crevice of them. But love must be turned from instinct into action. And that is what we see Rochester do. He describes the feeling of love, of wanting to bend Jane to his will with nothing more than his finger and his thumb, but then he turns that feeling of love into an intention and action of well wishes.

So many feelings of love get lost in translation. Horrible things are done in the name of love. And horrible things are asked to be forgiven with the words "But I love you." Rochester was guilty of this. He was ready to legally consume Jane without telling her the truth that their marriage would never be valid because he was already married. But here he draws the line and says, I will not tell you of my love, but I will actually wish good for you. He taxonomizes his love, saying, The possessiveness of my love makes me want to consume you. But the intention and action of my love forces me to let you go.

I love this scene and I can't always understand why. It is not a situation I find myself in frequently. When I left Peter it wasn't because the world was tearing us apart. It was because we misunderstood each other at a difficult moment. But, of course, I imagine the women who suffocated their crying babies so the Gestapo wouldn't find them and their older children. I imagine the people at the US-Mexican border who leave their families behind in order to try to make enough money for them to survive, only to be arrested. I see some of the moments that happen each day when someone knows exactly what they want, knows that they would be willing to do anything for it, and knows that there is nothing to do, and so they find the strength to do nothing.

Sheila Heti wrote in her book *Motherhood*, "Whether I want children is a secret I keep from myself. It is the biggest secret I keep from myself." And that's how I feel about having kids too—it's like I must know on some level. But it is the definition of ambivalence for me. Part of me wants it with my whole body. And another part of me is like, "Oh my God, it will destroy me. It will actually kill me." Not the pregnancy, but the tedium and the finances and the "What if I don't like it" and "What if she's sick" and "What if I have it right in the middle of the pandemic" and "What if it's an asshole" and "Won't it be so boring" and "Won't she ruin my career and my travel plans and break my back?" And I know that for a woman who has an ambition to learn and study and travel and hike miles, kids are everything good and are also roots that tie you to the earth.

I try to taxonomize myself and I can to some extent. Uterus is pro. Bank account is against. Heart is pro. Brain is against. Fears of being alone when I age are pro. Climate change fears are against. But what I lack is Jane's and Rochester's knack for figuring out who the prevailing expert is. If I had a baby, I would love her, and I could ask her. But that seems like a bad reason to have a kid, just to find out whether I really wanted one to begin with.

What I love about love, more than its well wishes, is its single-mindedness. You can love many things, but to love something unconditionally is to be able to properly separate from it. How can I love the idea of a baby and separate myself from it? That would lead me to never having a baby.

But then again, that is what Rochester does. This deeply loving act of not raping her releases Jane into extreme danger. She doesn't get not-raped to hug him good-bye and go live a safe, lovely life somewhere else. She knows that if she were to stay another night in Thornfield she would not be able to resist Rochester. Jane steals out in the middle of the night, forgets her money in a coach, and nearly starves to death after Rochester doesn't rape her. She gets saved and finds salvation, but by luck and only after great suffering. And it could have gone the other way as easily as it went the way it did.

Love is good intention. Love is acting well, from a place of wishing well. Love is wanting to consume but abstaining. "Whether I want kids is a secret I keep from myself," Sheila Heti says. And Rochester answers, "What good would it do . . . Conqueror I might be of the house, but the inmate would escape to heaven before I could call myself possessor of its clay dwelling-place." And I steal out into the night, and pray to end up somewhere safe.

CHAPTER ELEVEN

On Betrayal

Well, ma'am, afterwards the house was burnt to the ground:
there are only some bits of walls standing now.

—Chapter 36, *Jane Eyre*

After I had been reading *Jane Eyre* as sacred with Stephanie Paulsell for a while, she suggested that I start a "*Jane Eyre* as a sacred text*" reading group. I had been reading the book every day for more than a year, carrying it with me everywhere I went, along with my keys, wallet, and cell phone. I took it to the gym, to all my classes, to my various jobs. It had literally become part of my baggage.

Our reading group met every week for a semester. It was me and four other women; one of them was a friend named Ingrid, but the other three women were strangers to me who had read about the class in our humanist congregation's newsletter. When we gathered at our weekly meetings we would pore over a single passage from *Jane Eyre* for an hour at a time. We had often met without electricity, due to the relentless storms that followed our group's Tuesday nights like an omen. We'd stay in our coats, in an atheist Sunday school room, and wonder about things like why we love Jane so much and if Rochester is forgivable.

For our group's last meeting I decided to throw a bit of a party. So we ended in my dorm room on a lovely spring night. I was still living as a proctor, similar to an RA, but I was in my thirties, in the middle of Harvard Yard with thirty-four freshmen.

I met the three women who could attend the last session of our group on Memorial Church's steps. Memorial Church and its great hall is in the center of Harvard Yard, and this large building was built in memory of all the Harvard men who died in World War I. It has since become a continuous memorial to all Harvard students who die in war. It has all the Harvardian history one could possibly want associated with it; chapels built for benefactors, famous speakers who have blessed its walls with their words (some wise, some less so), and dead young people are all encompassed in its four walls. We gathered and then walked the five yards to my dorm.

Settled into my place, we passed around the homemade cup-
cakes that one of the women had brought, the homemade cookies that another had brought, and the tea supplies that I had on
my one-shelf "kitchen." For our last time together we watched
ridiculous scenes from the Orson Welles movie version of the
novel, which mostly features Welles shaking the woman who
plays Jane and then staring off meaningfully into the distance.
We laughed and debated our last *Jane* debates. These three
strangers had come to mean a lot to me; for who they were but
also because they had gone on an important adventure with me.
They had validated that Jane was worth spending a lot of time
with. They thought she was too, and voted with their bodies,
week after week, through snowstorm after snowstorm. They
kept me in practice with Jane, which after a year and with
Stephanie no longer available to me, I doubt I would have kept
up on my own. While the subway shut down and Harvard
classes were canceled for the first time in eighteen trillion years
or whatever, we sat there and we contemplated Jane's character,
life, and decisions together. This was a hearty, dedicated, beautiful little group, and I was feeling sentimental about saying
good-bye to them.

And now, as we were sitting in my dorm room saying good-
bye, two issues seemed to be still on everyone's minds: the
death of Bertha, the famous "madwoman in the attic," which is

violent and awful and uses the words "bashed brains," which come out of nowhere; and the very end of the novel, where St. John, the white male Christian missionary, somehow gets the last word instead of our heroine and narrator, Jane. None of us could really make sense of either of these facts. Why poor Bertha, who has been locked in a tower for more than ten years, gets her head smashed on the cobblestone after setting Thornfield Hall on fire and jumping to her death. And why our dear Jane doesn't give herself the final word and instead hands it to a man who is a bully and off in some British colony, trying to convert poor, unsuspecting people of color.

And in listening to the brilliant conversation that was unfolding, it occurred to me that a possible reason we were all tripping over these two moments in the novel is because both of them are moments in which great injustices are being done. We all loved this novel. That's why we were there. And I had asked everyone to treat the novel as sacred. And we are all predisposed to want to find good in things we love. We are predisposed to believe Tom Brady when he says that he just likes his footballs deflated because he's such a good quarterback, or bring up that George Washington freed his slaves in his will. We like to love what we love in uncomplicated ways. And in this moment, our group's last session together, we were coming up against our faith in the novel as a force for good. We were being confronted with two female victims: Bertha, who it was becoming clearer to me each time I read about her that she was a "passing" person of color, who is violently thrown away in the novel; and Jane, who, even when telling her own six-hundred-page story, cannot help but have her voice subsumed by the voice of a man who had tried to ruin her life by saying that he knew the will of God. And that meant this novel that I had been praying with for a year and a half, that I had carried on my back for miles and miles, that I had publicly preached on, is partially a racist argument for global imperialism, slavery, patriarchy, and missionaries. How did I end up here? I sat in silence wondering as the group kept discussing. How did I lead us here?

Over the next few days the full extent of my new understanding of the underbelly of this novel really settled in. I had led these women . . . *me!* I had led these wonderful women through a novel that is making the argument that all brown souls need to be saved by Christianity and that if they cannot be saved, then the brown people will wreak havoc on the lives of good Christians and must be sacrificed so that white (male) Christians can live their lives in the light, sure of divine rewards in the next life, lives of great churches and halls and feasts and wealth in this one. I had been treating as sacred a novel that argued that women will have their heads bashed on cobblestones, or not be given the last word of their own stories, while white men of wealth will have their names inscribed on buildings for posterity.

I didn't say as much in that reading group meeting on that beautiful spring night in my dorm room. It would have been a terrible way to end the class. And the despair that I was feeling wasn't the experience of the novel that this group of women had. I didn't say anything because although this ugliness had begun to dawn on me, I couldn't articulate it yet—certainly not clearly enough to say aloud. Besides, the book is about eighteen hundred other things as well. And the women probably already knew everything that was only just now occurring to naive little old me. I also didn't say anything because at the end of the day I was trained as a Jewish atheist but by a Christian preacher, and so I was trained to believe it is important to end journeys on a note of hope.

But during those days and weeks of contemplation after our meeting, waves of fear, almost panic, came over me: What had I put at the center of my life? What had I carried on my back all these months? What other naive things do I go around talking about as if they are great? Doubt consumed me.

We have all had these moments. Moments in which ugliness is all too suddenly revealed and knocks us over with its sheer force: betrayals. We have all been betrayed.

The precondition for betrayal is trust. You cannot be betrayed by something or someone that you did not at one time trust. Some betrayals are small—the friend who forgot your birthday even though you always remember theirs. The bus that doesn't stop for you on your morning commute. And you get over those quickly. You go right back to trusting the friend (they are so busy right now!) and the bus system (because usually it does stop for you; it must have been overcrowded). But then there are the big betrayals, the ones that, for a time, feel unendurable: the doctor who doesn't pay close enough attention and misdiagnoses you; the partner who cheats; the company you have given your all to that lets you go; the body that loses the baby it was supposed to grow and nourish. The only way to avoid feeling betrayed in your life is to avoid trusting, and to avoid trusting on that level would not only be deeply damaging, it would be impossible. The ground can betray you by shaking and cracking open; it would be shattering to stop trusting the ground.

Before we get too far into what we do when we feel betrayed, how we get to action, how we get to healing, how we get to hope (which we have established that I like to end with), let us talk for a moment about how hard betrayal feels. I don't want to skip that discussion, because it's important to remember that this is a lonely experience but a universal one. And if we get to hope too quickly it will only be what the theologian Dietrich

Bonhoeffer calls "cheap grace." And we all know that buying something cheap means it may get us through for a short time but ultimately it falls apart fast. I promise I'll try to get us to hope. That's my goal. That's my training. But I'm going to try to gently go through the pain and not pretend it doesn't exist.

When I have been betrayed, one of the main feelings is embarrassment, as if I have been taken for being stupid or actually been stupid. I feel as though I have been taken as a fool, and worst of all, I feel as though I cannot trust myself anymore. I had trusted whatever it was and it wasn't worthy of my trust. So I begin to panic: What else have I falsely put my trust in and what else will turn out to be a lie? It feels like even gravity is up for discussion. The world suddenly appears to be chaos, and any sense of control evaporates into the illusion that I know in theory it always is, but that I rarely live as my day-to-day experience.

This moment I had with *Jane Eyre* was a betrayal, and I felt so stupid. I had chosen this book to put at the center of my life. I had chosen it because the Bible was too tainted. I had chosen it intentionally and all on my own. I chose it because I loved it and my mother had loved it before me and generations of readers before her. It felt like a safe book to love and to center my life around, unlike the Bible, with its two-thousand-plus years of baggage. And I had talked so publicly about its virtues. But it is indefensible the extent to which *Jane Eyre* is racist and patriarchal.

There is a cheap-grace way out of the pain that this betrayal caused. I could say, "I guess nothing can be treated as sacred; nothing bears up to scrutiny. Nothing is truly worth worshipping. I gave it my best try." But that's cynicism, and I don't want to get more and more cynical. As I mentioned earlier, the only way to avoid betrayal is to avoid trusting. I don't want to be that person, the person who trusts nothing and no one. I have a vision of the type of old person I want to be and she hasn't become cynical; she's awesome. She travels and has eight dogs and she's tough but not because she has rough edges due to all the chips on her shoulders.

So eventually, out of sheer lack of options, I went back to the thing that I trusted, *Jane Eyre*, to see if it was the answer to the problem it had caused. I couldn't tell if I was acting out of faith or if it was the choice of a true addict. But in returning to the novel, I remembered that it wasn't that I had set out to trust it. My thesis in this experiment was not that *Jane Eyre* was sacred in and of itself but that if I treated something as sacred, it could be sacred. My trust was in my ability to treat something as sacred and for it to teach me if I did so. And so I went back and trusted that fact, decoupled it from the text again. The act and the thing had gotten their roots tangled, so it took some time for me to untangle them. But eventually I was able to go back to the thing I had committed to—not what I was hurt by, but what I had believed when I was, as Jane might say, "quite sane." I went back to being experimentally certain that she would have something positive to say to me if I kept in conversation with her, and didn't just shut her out when she disappointed me.

What I eventually realized, once I had begun to trust the process again, was that I had been missing a point that I had been rubbing up against for a while. I had been trying to learn from Jane when really I should have been learning from Bertha, that madwoman in the attic who gets her brains bashed in on the sidewalk. I do not want to live like Jane, who at the end of the novel gives up her own voice for a Christian missionary to get the final word. I want to be Bertha: the woman who burns down the symbol of patriarchy on my way out.

Bertha gets three paragraphs in the entire novel in which she is on the page and is actively in the scene. Given that she is the major plot twist of the novel, three scanty paragraphs seems reductive at best. She is described as having a purple face and bloated features. She does not have hair but "shaggy locks." She is violent and is constantly trying to attack people. And after *Jane Eyre*, the novel, betrayed me, I can say more assuredly than ever that I love Bertha Mason Rochester passionately and with a complete commitment.

Bertha, like me, has a history of vague and mixed ethnicity and a familial history of mental illness. I also have long, shaggy locks and eyes with red on them due to melanin. I have let her into my heart entirely. She has entered my imagination completely. I preached a sermon on the book of Acts, chapter three, and spoke of almost nothing but Bertha. Since my betrayal by *Jane Eyre*, I see Bertha everywhere.

Every other character in *Jane Eyre* gets their due. Helen Burns, the saintlike child and Jane's first real friend, dies in bed being held by her best friend, warm, well loved, and sure of her ascension into heaven. Aunt Reed, the abusive, manipulative guardian of Jane, dies in pain, desperate and miserable. Edward Rochester, the good man who locked a woman in an attic for ten years and almost made an unknowing mistress of Jane, gets maimed and blinded, only to have his sight restored when he finds God. St. John, the noble missionary and martyr, dies on a mission, sure of God's will and his own place in God's plan.

Only Bertha Mason Rochester, the "mad wife," gets an ending that is unaccounted for. Bertha is the only character whose fate is borne out in the novel and whose spiritual life is never described or even alluded to. Bertha ends with her brains splattered on cobblestone and no reckoning with her maker is discussed. Jane finds out about Bertha's death from a local innkeeper, who starts the following dialogue. She is told that, most likely, Bertha set the house on fire and was on the roof as the flames engulfed the mansion. Mr. Rochester made sure that everyone else in the house was safe and then:

"Mr. Rochester ascend through the sky-light on to the roof; we heard him call 'Bertha!' We saw him approach her; and then, ma'am, she yelled and gave a spring, and the next minute she lay smashed on the pavement."

"Dead?"

"Dead! Ay, dead as the stones on which her brains and blood were scattered."

"Good God!"

"You may well say so, ma'am: it was frightful!"

He shuddered.

"And afterwards?" I urged.

"Well, ma'am, afterwards the house was burnt to the ground: there are only some bits of walls standing now."

"Were any other lives lost?"

While other people's deaths get literally pages of explanation and commentary, Bertha's death is not even the main focal point of its description. We hear of Rochester's heroism and what happened afterward and then quickly move on to finding out whether anyone else died too. She is simply "smashed on the pavement" and "dead as the stones on which her brains and blood were scattered." In a novel that ends with the words "Lord Jesus!" this is the epitome of a secular death, and I am sure in my bones that Bertha's death is so secular because she is Black and mad. Her death is gross, distasteful, and "frightful" to those who had to see it. But it is just another sacrifice. It is just another death of a Black woman who was used for her wealth to build up nations like England. It does not need to be reckoned with in the context of the novel.

The questions that most readers are led to when they contemplate Bertha are ones that I struggled with as well: Is she a monster? Is she merely a plot device? Or is Brontë asking her readers to wonder about Rochester's wife, wonder what drove her mad, wonder if he would one day lock up Jane if she began to show signs of "madness"? Is Bertha a comment on capitalism and slavery? Is she a comment on women's role in the nineteenth century and how they felt? I think I've even lost track of what question I am supposed to be asking here, because Bertha causes me to doubt the humanity of Charlotte Brontë's project. I am not sure if Brontë is intentionally demonstrating to us that the only way countries like England were built was with the sacrifices and unaccounted-for deaths of endless invisible people. And if she is not doing that on purpose, then she is just

doing the same thing as countries like England: she is sacrific-
ing the invisible person for the plot of a Romance novel.

Bertha is the truly gothic part of this experiment for me. She
is alive for me, she is a monster for me, and she is a ghost who
haunts me. She shows me that I breathed life into a novel that
is comfortable with brains on cobblestones. She is a reminder of
the fact that I buy cheap clothes that I know are made by slaves
and am sort of just fine with that. She is a reminder of every
time I have ever compromised my principles in order to get
something I want—the times I have let a man treat me badly,
the times I have forgiven myself too easily for a ratty transgres-
sion, the times I have not mustered the energy to be kind or
have willpower.

Bertha does not need to have meaning read into her on the
page. Now that she is alive, it is my relationship with her that
has meaning.

If I believe in *Jane Eyre* as scripture, there is nothing wrong
with seeing Bertha not as a fleshed-out character but as a metaphor, as an allegorical rendering of everything that must be
sacrificed in order for the Christian world of hands fairly dealt
to exist.

There is even an entirely vivid photograph of Bertha and me
in my head. I have an imaginary version of it framed on my
wall by my bed next to the photos of my closest friends and

family members. In this imaginary photo, Bertha is sitting with her dark skin, her red eyes, and her thick, dark locks, in a dirty, thick, long white nightgown on a curb outside Memorial Church. I am sitting there just a few feet away from her, because she's dangerous and might hurt me, and also because she does not like it when I get too close. But we sit next to each other on the curb in companionable silence.

The church doors are open and the reason I have framed this fictional photograph of her and me is because someone glorious was preaching inside that day, the day the fictional photo was taken. Someone who gets that the church is the only possible answer to suffering and should be burned to the ground because it does not offer a satisfying answer. Someone who knows that the only thing to do when a woman is locked in an attic for ten years is pray for her and knows that prayer is an insulting response to her suffering. Someone who knows that the word *God* cannot be reclaimed for the rational, to be used only to mean the good versions of what God means, but also knows that there is no other word for that elusive thing. That preacher is why this photo matters. But that preacher is not in the photo. Because Bertha and I can't go into that church. She is not sufficiently accounted for in the prayers that talk about redemption and neither was my family in Auschwitz. The best of the church, and there are many of them, reach out to us. But the walls of history and failures, while not a barrier to everyone, are a barrier to us. And therefore, until we feel appropriately accounted for, we sit on the curb, just outside, voting with our bodies that we do not abide by what is going on in there. In the picture we are both looking at the ground, seemingly absorbed in the asphalt. You wouldn't even know that there was someone speaking inside or that we were listening intently. It looks like we were only accidentally hearing some of the things being preached, while tracing invisible drawings onto the pavement. Bertha would be outside because she would know that there is no concept of God that is complete enough to include her in it. And I would sit out there because there is no concept of God that is complete enough to include her in it. She symbolizes everyone and everything for me that is not accounted for in the church. Bertha is sacred to me.

I understand why most people identify with Jane and not Bertha. I did. And I forgive myself for falling into that trap. In defense of those of us who identify with Jane, she ends up happily married, independently wealthy, and living in some sort of Keebler elf romantic bungalow with everyone she loves visiting constantly, and she gets all this through trying to be a good person. And it's not like Jane's this glorious, unattainable heroine. The whole schtick about Jane is that she is "poor, plain and little." We mere mortals are invited to see ourselves in her.

But after my betrayal, when I went back to the thing that I trusted, the idea that if you keep treating something as sacred—not believing that it is sacred but treating it *as if* it was sacred—I realized that if you keep looking at something, if you keep working hard at something you cherish, it will keep giving you gifts, and Bertha is my latest gift. Unlike Jane's glorified ending, Bertha burnt the whole house down with her. I don't believe in martyrdom, but as far as a metaphor to look further into, as far as badassery, as far as an act of rebellion rather than submission, I am totally into that.

I am humbler now about my love of Jane and skeptical of anything that I begin to love with too much fervor. But without the betrayal I never would have seen the beauty of the madwoman in the attic. It wasn't the thing that I believed in that betrayed me. It was that I lost sight of what I believed in. I never set out to believe that *Jane Eyre* was perfect. I sought to believe that if I treated the novel as sacred, it would give me blessings. And that has always been true.

Betrayals make us feel as though we cannot trust the world. In extreme cases, that might be justified. But often we can find the gift if we look for it. Go back and wonder about what it was that you really trusted. Did you trust that your partner would never mess up, or did you trust the idea that loyalty is possible? Go back. Not to dwell on the betrayal, not to trust the person who cheated on you, but to trust what it was that you believed in again. Not to forget that your body once betrayed you, but to trust that there are ways in which your body still serves you and to honor those ways. Don't go back to the bad doctor, but believe that trusting medical professionals who are good at their jobs can be useful. You have to go back to the thing you trusted. Don't go to the trauma but to the thing that made you believe.

Because you trusted it for a reason. Go back. That's how you relearn to trust yourself. You are forgiving yourself; you are teaching yourself that you survive and that you are optimistic. You are going back to hope.

And if you can't get back to hope, then in the meantime, there is room on the curb with me and Bertha.

My grandmother went to bed one day and only got out of bed a year later. I told you that story. The story I didn't tell you was how she got out of bed. It goes like this:

Papa was excited to see the film *The Diary of Anne Frank* when it came out in 1959. He insisted that Mama go with him. It was a production to get her dressed. He had to carry her to the car from the bed, and then hold her as she walked the few steps from the car to the movie theater. They sat and watched the movie together. As they were leaving, my grandfather held her as she made her way back to the car, and she said to him, "You can let go. I can walk." And she could.

CHAPTER TWELVE

On the Afterlife in *Little Women*

I'm not afraid, but it seems as if I should be homesick
for you even in heaven.

—Chapter 36, *Little Women*

I have shed too many tears over Beth March. Granted that I am obviously a person who is highly affected by art. For example, the only moment in my life when I was completely convinced that I wanted to be a mom was the first time I saw the song performed at the end of *Mamma Mia! Here We Go Again*, when the ghost of Meryl Streep comes back and sings to her daughter that she was the love of her life. I know that according to the Kabbalah, God counts the tears of women. But I am sort of wondering if God stopped counting my tears around 1995, a year after the release of the first *Little Women* movie I saw, when I became obsessed.

Part of me hopes that God does not count my Beth tears. Because I've cried more for Beth March than I have for the girls who were kidnapped by Boko Haram, or for polar bears starving to death. I've cried more for Beth March over the years than I did when my own grandmother died. I hope that the God I don't believe in doesn't notice the imbalance and knows that the tears I did cry for my grandmother were more important tears. But I obviously also think the Beth March and *Mamma Mia!* tears should count, because I hope that when I cry for Beth March, I am in part crying for kidnapped girls and my grandmother. Catharsis, right? My Beth March tears aren't just about Beth March, I hope.

But here's the thing: the Beth March death is so sad, even without its cathartic elements. And it is sad because Beth does not want to die, even though she believes in heaven.

For those of you who don't know or cannot remember, Beth March is one of the four March sisters in the Louisa May Alcott classic, *Little Women*. I have cried over her death the five or so times I have read the novel. And I have cried over her death the dozens of times I have watched Claire Danes's beautiful chin quiver, playing Beth in the 1994 film adaptation of the book. Beth gets very sick with scarlet fever as a little girl. She beats it, but according to one physician friend I have spoken to, her heart is weakened; she dies several years later, most likely due to complications from rheumatic fever. She is around twenty-three years old when she dies, and she knew for many months before that she was dying. Two of her sisters are far away when Beth gets very sick, and she insists that neither of them should be called home to spend her last months with her. But Jo, her favorite sister, comes home anyway.

The brutal scene in the book takes place at the sea. Jo takes Beth there with money she has earned from teaching and writing so that Beth can get strong. It is here that Beth tells Jo that she knows she won't get strong, that she knows she is dying and has come to terms with it. It is supposed to be a trip in which Jo is taking care of Beth. But it turns into a trip in which Beth is taking care of Jo.

That inverse is always enough to bring me to my knees. After I accidentally step on my dog's paw she will run to me to make me feel better, to tell me that she knows I didn't do it on purpose. And I cry when she does that. Anytime the weaker one is trying to take care of the stronger one, it flattens me. And it, of course, makes me wonder if maybe my dog and Beth are actually the strong ones and Jo and I are both just blustering blowhards.

In the one scene in particular that gets to me, there is a line that is always my breaking point. Until I hear or read this line, I can almost convince myself that this will be the time I won't shed a single Beth March tear. But then the line comes and I prove once again to be a cliché of myself.

The moment is when Beth says to Jo, who is maybe her favorite person in the world, "I'm not afraid, but it seems as if I should be homesick for you even in heaven." The fact that Beth loves Jo so much that even in her most perfect vision of an afterlife she cannot imagine not missing Jo is always what puts me over the edge. Or that maybe part of Beth's idea of perfection is missing Jo, because as long as Beth is missing her, Jo is still alive. Which means that Beth values life and is therefore sad to leave it.

But what is even sadder is another reading of that line. Maybe it is that Beth can imagine a heaven without missing Jo, but chooses to say to Jo anyway, "I will miss you, even in heaven," as a way of trying to convey to Jo the depth of her love. All of these possible readings have racked up many tears on my counter. Mostly what makes me weep is the certainty that those I love will die. If Beth can die, any of us, it turns out, can and probably will.

Not believing in the afterlife is fundamental to my understanding of who I am. I don't just not believe in the afterlife. I believe that the afterlife often is a tool of oppression and an instrument of evil. I believe that its most common use is to keep the oppressed in their place. Promises of a kingdom of heaven make toil on behalf of the powerful more palatable in this life and makes revolution feel less necessary and urgent.

Not believing in the afterlife is essential to my understanding of myself as a person and as a chaplain. Not believing in the afterlife is what keeps me able to sit with people in their suffering when that is what they need from me.

I was a brand-new chaplain, still not really sure what it meant to have my vocation, when my friend Mike called me late one night. Mike had just found out that his mother, who a week ago had seemed to everyone to be perfectly healthy, was actually not only dying of cancer but had less than a month to live. He called because he said that if one more person said to him, "She's going to a better place," he'd lose it. He was calling his atheist friend, who didn't believe his mom was going to a better place. He called not because he agreed with me. He said clearly that he didn't know how he felt about the afterlife. But he called me because he didn't want to think about the idea of his mom going to a better place right now. He wanted to think about how much he was going to miss her on this earth. I said, "I'm so sorry. This sucks." I don't think I said much else.

This is how I understand my vocation, as the person you can come to when you just want someone to say: That sucks. I don't think things will be fine and I don't think everything happens for a reason. If you want someone who will sit with you in that space, even when for you it is just a way station, that's fine. That is what I am here for. I live in that way station.

And what I love so much about Beth is that she is saying,

Even in the best possible circumstances, even if there is a heaven and I get into it, I will miss you, Jo. And so she is saying, The fact that I am dying . . . well, it sucks. And Jo, I will sit with you here on this beach and keep you company while you let it sink in how much this sucks. I'm dying; we are going to miss each other and it will not be fine."

There was one day in my whole life when I enjoyed thinking not quite about the afterlife but about a next life. I have the same problem with next lives as I have with afterlives: they make justice far too murky in this one. Karma does not come back around; some people just get to be bad their whole lives and die self-satisfied. And others are good their whole lives and die in mental, physical, and psychological anguish. Those, as far as I'm concerned, are the facts. Reincarnation distorts the bleakness of this truth.

But there was one day when a next life appeared very quickly in front of me. I was walking with one of my best friends, Julia. We had set ourselves a big hiking task of more than twenty miles that day. We were walking half of the Wicklow Way, an old Irish trail. We had started in Dublin the day before, and in two days we would have hiked our way to Glendalough. Four days to walk from Dublin to Glendalough, and a one-hour bus ride would take us back. Walks like this are made for thinking, singing Motown, and feeling inspired by the tens of thousands of people who have walked this path before you and the majesty of this place. It is also grueling—so grueling that you might as well start thinking about the afterlife, even if you hate the idea of an afterlife.

We were walking through low heather, which was covered in thousands of spiderwebs with dew-laced rainbows bouncing off them. We found ourselves approaching a forest ahead when I said to Julia that I wanted to come back as a tree in my next life. I realized it was true as it came out of my mouth. Looking at those gorgeous trees starting so abruptly, in a line straight in front of us, in Ireland, thousands of miles away from where I had met Julia, made me so happy to be exactly where I was. It was stunning to see a forest begin, one tree at a time and so suddenly. And that threshold simultaneously made me feel two things. First, I felt wholeheartedly homesick for the trees of California; the sequoias, oaks, and redwoods of my childhood. I genuinely longed for the trees that taught me what trees are, that taught me how to think about time (redwoods that live for one thousand years and that I have seen ripped up at the roots in a bad, sudden storm), about the environment, and about hospitality. Second, I felt so glad to be far away from where I had come from, glad that I was free enough to travel and see so much of the world.

Walking in Ireland that day, I suddenly had a whole fantasy.

I wanted to spend one hundred years as a redwood. I wanted to house birds and watch them hatch and then leave. I think squirrels are disgusting, but I would host them in my branches, even as they broke parts of me, making idiotic jumps for no real reason. I wanted people to read in my shade and marvel at the beauty in their lives because of my height. A bad psychologist would say that it's my five-foot-three stature that probably makes me yearn to be the world's tallest tree. But fuck that fictional psychologist. I, in the middle of nowhere, seven thousand miles away from home, wanted to be rooted to the ground for one hundred years, which suddenly felt like a very short amount of time.

Looking back, I think that being happy about where I was and yet longing so hard to be home made me think of a version of an afterlife—an afterlife that I don't believe in. Right then Beth's line, "I know I will be lonesome for you, even in heaven," began to recite itself in my mind. I think that is what Beth is trying to convince Jo her afterlife experience will be. "Don't worry about me. It will be blissful. But I will still yearn for you. In fact, it will in part be the bliss that will make me yearn for you."

I love several things about what Beth implies in her confession. I love the idea that there are certain things on this earth that even heaven can't get right, that are better here for their mortality. There are things on this earth that are more beautiful because of their brevity—the band playing on as the *Titanic* sinks, and one's relationship with a beloved sister. And there are things on earth that suck for their shortness, like the band playing on as the *Titanic* sinks and one's relationship with a beloved sister.

So yes, I hate the afterlife because I think it has often been used to keep the vulnerable on the margins. But I also hate it for taking the focus away from this beautiful life that it sucks to leave. The afterlife makes the moments when I watch my stepdaughter and Peter put together a puzzle with delight less gorgeous. And I love their gorgeousness. And I love how much it sucks that it won't go on like this forever.

The reason we cry over Beth is because she is so earthbound. She doesn't want to leave the house. The first time she is sick, she is made well by her mother coming home. She cannot possibly want to go to heaven. She loves hearth—her piano, dolls, earthly things. She loves her sisters and kittens and purple eyes. And the idea of Beth going anywhere is just more than we can bear.

We don't want Beth to die because Beth, really, doesn't want to die. She tells us that she is ready to be brave, like Jo. And that she is excited to finally be the one who is leaving everyone else behind, after they have all and always left her behind. But we know in our bones that these are the justifications of the doomed. Beth is the person who tells us through quivering lips that they are glad to have been dumped—relieved, really.

What we wish instead for Beth is what I wish for all believers: that her wishes would have been made true on earth. Beth wanted her sisters to be home with her and for them to be happy to be home. She wanted to be frozen in a time when it would always have been okay to feed dolls and when her neighbors wouldn't have been so poor. She wishes she could play piano every day. She wishes that the Hummels had never been so poor that she had needed to go over and take care of them and catch scarlet fever from them in the fucking first place. What she wanted was a humble heaven on earth. And she feels the loss of having to settle for an ethereal heaven instead.

Charlie Hallisey, a teacher of mine at divinity school, tells a story that a Buddhist priest friend of his told him. It is a story about a Japanese mom whose son was dying. The son told her that it was all right that he was dying, that they would meet each other again in the Western Paradise (the Pure Land of Pure Land Buddhism—not heaven, exactly, but an afterlife). And after he died, she told the Buddhist priest, "I don't even believe in the Pure Land. But I have to get there now."

For the record, if there were a heaven, it would be one in which everyone I loved could come back as redwood trees near each other. I think what I really want is to spend a few hundred years as a redwood, housing birds and squirrels, having branches fall off in storms, watching humanity mess up from a distance, and feeling nothing but love and compassion for the world. I think I could muster a terrible amount of compassion if I were a redwood. And I'm grateful for the imaginative nature of next- and afterlife conversations, because otherwise it might not ever occur to me to think of the perspective of a redwood—and I think I have been made better by thinking through that perspective.

I am, of course, a liar. Greta Gerwig's 2019 version of *Little Women* didn't have this line of "I should be homesick for you even in heaven." And I still cried my Beth March tears. And I hope that the God I don't believe in counts those tears too.

CHAPTER THIRTEEN

On Hope in *Harry Potter*

Their presence was his courage.

—Chapter 34, *Harry Potter and the Deathly Hallows*

When I worked as a congregational chaplain, a small part of my job was hospital visits. I would visit a member of our congregation if they'd had surgery or needed chemotherapy. We had one member of our congregation, whom I will call Anne, who was about twenty-five years old, and was also part of our *Harry Potter and the Sacred Text* reading group. I liked her. She was sincere and bright, kind and always willing to help. She showed up every week to our reading group with a smile, with something smart to say, always talking to the new person and being incredibly inclusive in a gracious way that often felt elusive to me. She even always volunteered to do the most thankless job during our class time: hold the basket for donations as people left class each week and silently shake them down for their two bucks. And she was in and out of the hospital a lot.

When Anne was young, she was playing around with friends, roughhousing the way many of us did in childhood, and she broke her hip. She has had more than a dozen surgeries on her hip since then and none of them have worked; several of them have made her condition worse.

Sometimes the pain would get so bad that Anne would need to go to the hospital for acute pain management. Her muscles would spasm visibly through her clothes. Although she would not directly contact me, sometimes I would find out one way or another and go to visit her in the emergency room or her hospital room.

I was all frantic energy on those visits. I would read her sections of the Harry Potter books. I would chat with her about her love life and show her pictures of my dog. I would advocate for her when nurses didn't keep their promises to be back soon, politely popping my head out, understanding that the nurses were waiting for the doctors, who almost definitely weren't just sitting around doing nothing, but still I gently demanded some attention for my ward. Sometimes the pain would be so bad that tears would simply be streaming silently down Anne's cheeks as I tried my very best to distract her, like a kid trying to end a fight she doesn't understand between her parents.

I am not a seasoned hospital chaplain. But I've done a good bit of training and am not a total novice either. In most hospital-visit experiences, you meet someone after they have been checked into the hospital. The first time you see them they are either terrified in the emergency room or they are in their gowns already. To me, their whole identities were those of sick people. I never saw them without IVs in their arms that prevented them from fixing their hair. I never saw them being good at their jobs or kind to their children or yelling at a driver who cut them off.

So chaplaincy visits with these people were acute care. I got to read their charts ahead of time, which had every private detail about them. When I met them, I had all the authority in the room. I am convinced that IVs are not just to keep people medicated or hydrated but are also designed in part so that patients feel psychologically tied to their beds. And so a typical chaplaincy visit in a hospital involves someone tied to their bed, while I am walking around, moving chairs, and the picture of health. Because they are strangers, I get to ask them direct questions like, "Are you scared?" or "Where are you finding comfort and support while you are here?" And as soon as I say, "I am the chaplain," some people kick me out, but others immediately tell me their whole hearts. Once, my entire interaction with a patient involved my being called into her room right after she had been given a horrible diagnosis. She was having a panic attack and so the doctor was going to get her some sort of sedative. I held her hand for about five seconds as she looked into my eyes and said, "I have two children." Then the doctor was back with nurses in tow and my job was done. I never saw her again. Once, a patient asked me, "What can you do for me?" And the only honest answer that occurred to me was, "Well, I am just about the only person who will walk into this room who won't poke you and who you can kick out." She invited me to take a seat. We chatted about TV.

But visiting Anne was different from any of my training. She wasn't just a patient but was a person I knew who happened to now be in the hospital, a totally different chaplaincy and one in which I was a virgin. I knew her as someone who came to our book group and so I felt uncomfortable asking her direct, personal questions. I didn't want her to feel like she had overshared and then stop coming to our Wednesday classes, which I knew were a comfort to her. So I all but tap-danced for her. I told her funny stories to distract her from her pain rather than trying to engage with it. I once came straight from a date, still in heels and out of ideas as to what to talk about, and described to her how the date had gone. Boundaries are one of the most important facets of being a chaplain, and I ignored all that training when I was with Anne.

I know I sound like I was a horrible chaplain to Anne. And the truth is that I was. I studied to be a chaplain because I wanted to sit with people during the difficult moments in their lives and bear witness to the world's suffering—the very suffering that I think God turns away from. Anne made me realize that I didn't want to bear witness to people's suffering. I wanted to be available to bear witness to strangers' suffering. Knowing someone made it too difficult for me to look closely. Given that I knew Anne outside the hospital, I wanted her back in the world that I knew her in. So the toughest bit for me on those often late-night visits, other than seeing someone in pain, of course, was that I could not ever figure out how to leave. I would stay for hours and hours, waiting for someone to say something definitive, like, "Here is the treatment plan. These are the next three steps and this is how we will make it better." I kept waiting for a sign that our time together was over. And I could never quite find it.

Anne would say, "Vanessa, you can go. It could be hours."

And I would say, "I will leave soon. I just want to wait for you to see a doctor."

An hour later, with me yawning, she would say, "Vanessa, please feel free to go. It could be forever."

And still I would protest. I would ask again if I should read to her from *Harry Potter*, show her another photo of my dog, show her another YouTube video. But at the next yawn, she would insist.

"Go. There is nothing for you to wait for. They will give me pain meds or they won't. Please, just go."

That was her, trying to take care of me. And I would let her.

I would take her offer and gratefully finally feel free to leave. And even after she had done all that work to let me leave, I would compulsively find myself chattering away, trying to give a follow-up step, a plan. "I will call you in the morning, and hopefully the doctors will have said something useful and we'll have some next steps," I would say. Anne would smile and nod, knowing more than I. I had to leave her on a hopeful note. I had to. Not for her sake, but for mine. I somehow was incapable of leaving her without a plan, without a sign that things would be better. And she, bless her, after all her years of pain, of doctors accusing her of drug seeking, of failed surgeries, would soothe me, like Beth with Jo. Looking back, I wonder if Anne was taking care of herself too.

I rebelled against the reality that Anne had simply been in pain for more than half of her life and had come to terms with the fact that these hospital visits were just part of her experience. She did not like that they were a fact of her life and grieved the truth of it. But she had a life. She would struggle with work. With finding the right medications and treatments. She would have friends and would date and would apply to grad school. And all of it would be in pain.

Gradually, I lost hope for Anne, that she would ever be painfree. And as I came to that realization, I found myself less and less likely to go on hospital visits. I would go if she asked, but only if she asked. There was no more just showing up if I heard about it. After a year of these visits, I left my job as a congregational chaplain and Anne still was in and out of the hospital. Even though she could still use visits, even though I often knew when she was in the hospital, even though she once specifically asked me to come and my schedule would have allowed me to go, I didn't. I justified that I did not visit because it wasn't my job anymore, so the boundaries were blurry and going to see her would be unprofessional. Suddenly, boundaries were very important to me.

But the truth was, now that I had realized that there was no hope for Anne's situation, I didn't see the point of my visits anymore. It would never get better. I knew my visits would still help her. But I could not get myself to go. There was no goal to work toward; we weren't trying to get her better. We weren't just trying to make the last few months of her life comfortable and happy. She kept having surgeries, hoping this would be the one that worked, but it never was. The medical system was failing her and I couldn't stand to watch it anymore.

Harry Potter gets himself into a lot of situations that I would call hopeless throughout the entirety of the book series. When we meet him, he lives as a hostage in a cupboard under the stairs in the abusive home of his aunt and uncle. He faces Voldemort, the embodiment of evil, all alone as an eleven-year-old, and all that saves him is reaching into his pocket at the right moment. He gets locked in basement after basement, plunged into a dark maze, and sent night after night to a detention that he does not deserve, only to have to endure self-mutilation at the hands of a madwoman. And he always, through some sort of intervention, ingenuity, or sheer grit, manages to get himself out of these impossible situations—situations in which I would complain to the highest authority, scream bloody murder, or curl up and wait for death. Harry always endures and perseveres. He keeps wiggling around until something changes.

For Harry, the chosen boy wizard, hope in the face of hopelessness is nearly pathological. After enduring years of abuse at the Dursleys', he still makes jokes at their expense right in front of their faces, knowing that the smack will come. Even after Vernon has been keeping Harry's letters away from him for weeks, Harry still hopes that he will be able to grab one of the letters Hogwarts is sending him. And this hope is mostly rewarded for Harry, even to the point of divine intervention. Magical birds come and bring him back to life with healing tears, and necessary weapons appear at the bottoms of frozen lakes. Harry is able to do impossible things because he has been rewarded by the Fates rising to meet him every time he is brave and bold enough to keep hoping when most of us would give up.

I pride myself on not believing in divine intervention. I believe in grace, that sometimes good things show up as if from God even when we do not deserve them. But I do not believe in magic. I do not believe in a kind of grace that one can rely on. Terrible things happen and there is no justice, and that trope plays out all the time. It is important to me to remember this, lest I become too hopeful and forget to be angry and outraged at angering and outrageous things. Calling something by its proper name is important to me.

In "The Forest Again," a chapter found toward the very end of the entire Harry Potter series, the tone is different from the rest of the times Harry finds himself in these impossible situations. The hopelessness of the situation that Harry has found himself in at this point of the series is essential to the task itself, and much is made of that necessary hopelessness. Harry is being asked to sacrifice himself and is told that if it is not a complete sacrifice, then it will be insufficient for the magic to work. I think of this scene often. It is, of course, the scene in which Harry famously walks into the forest to die willingly by Voldemort's hand.

As he walks into the forest, Harry has to keep convincing himself to really be hopeless. The feeling that he could do one last thing to change his fate, to outsmart the situation, is so ingrained in him that he has to keep convincing himself that this moment is different from the rest of his life.

The text says, "Harry understood at last that he was not supposed to survive. His job was to walk calmly into Death's welcoming arms." Harry, as he walks, deeply resents this fate as it finally begins to sink in and as it becomes clearer and clearer to him. He resents that he knows it is coming. His death is by necessity an intentional, slow acquiescence, which goes against his very nature.

Harry begins to think in the metaphor of something that he has always loved, a quidditch game. The "game was ended, the Snitch had been caught, it was time to leave the air. . . ." It is then that Harry remembers that he has a Snitch with him that was left to him in Albus Dumbledore's will. It is the first Snitch that Harry ever caught and it is engraved with the short sentence "I open at the close." Harry reaches for the Snitch with "nerveless fingers."

The phrase "nerveless fingers" is perplexing. I think it is supposed to be saying that Harry fumbled with the Snitch—the first time ever that Harry would have struggled gripping something firmly where a Snitch is concerned. But I am not sure it is entirely clear that this is the only meaning we are meant to glean from the phrase "nerveless fingers." Nerves are what give you the ability to feel with your fingers. Nerves are what makes you feel anxious. Nerve is what gives you courage. It may be that all of these different kinds of nerves are gone in the face of the despair and fear that Harry is in the midst of in this moment. It might be that he has no feeling in his fingertips, no courage, no fear, no hope. All Harry is, is action.

It is with these nerveless fingers that Harry holds the Snitch and whispers to it, the most hopeless sentence possible: "I am about to die." Upon the revelation of this desperate admission, the Snitch opens, giving Harry the power to conjure the dead. And four dead people appear. The living cannot possibly comfort Harry at this moment. If Hermione or Ron were by his side, Harry would have to be like Anne was with me, taking care of the caretaker. Only the dead can help Harry now, and they come for him, the four people Harry most longs to speak to in the world: his mother, his father, Lupin, and Sirius.

It is at least a little remarkable that it is these four adults who appear, when it seems as though the criteria for this appearance is having loved Harry and being dead. Because the question is, of course, where is Dumbledore?

It is not explained why Dumbledore does not appear in this moment of complete crisis for his mentee. Instead, he appears in the next chapter, at King's Cross station, and I think there is a reason for this absence and later appearance.

I suspect Dumbledore does not show up at this moment because Harry "knew that [these four people] would not tell him to go, that it would have to be his decision." But Dumbledore might encourage Harry to keep walking, to hurry. Dumbledore, possibly, would not be offering comfort to Harry but encouraging action—the last thing that anyone needs in a hopeless situation. Maybe Dumbledore is not resurrected by the stone that came out of the Snitch because he would be tempted to give tactical advice when what Harry needs is comfort.

As Harry stands and looks at the people who loved him and who showed up for him even after they died, he does not ask for advice. He asks to be taken care of. He asks, "Does it hurt?" about dying. To which Sirius, someone Harry watched die, answers, "Quicker and easier than falling asleep." The adults do not instigate conversation; they wait to follow Harry's lead. No advice. No promise of an afterlife. No consoling. The only promise made is, again, in response to a direct request from Harry for his four beloved caretakers to "stay close." And James says, "Until the very end." And even that simple promise of intervention cannot be kept. When Harry is finally confronted with Voldemort, he drops the resurrection stone that has brought his four onlookers back to life, and so they disappear. He has to go alone to this last place.

After Harry goes to fight Voldemort, he wakes up in King's Cross station. It is there, at a crossroads in which Harry has to make a decision, that Dumbledore appears. Dumbledore the adviser, Dumbledore the mentor, Dumbledore the wise. He gives Harry advice and information because hope is now an option again. A new reality has presented itself to Harry, and in this new reality he needs something other than company; he needs a teacher again.

I'm not sure that Anne is quite walking through the forest. I suspect that she is sitting on the forest floor. But the issue that I am struggling with isn't really about Anne and what she is doing or where she is. Regardless of exactly where she is, I am sure that she is doing everything she can. She is doing everything right. The real question is how I get myself to be one of the invited ghosts for Anne, rather than Dumbledore, useless in the setting that she finds herself in time and time again. Anne does not need advice. She has doctors for that. Anne doesn't need me to make her feel better. She has nurses for that. Anne needs the presence modeled for me by Sirius, Lupin, James, and Lily. These ghostly four are comfortable with silence. They do not try to change anything. All they do is walk alongside and answer the questions posed directly to them honestly, keeping their answers as simple as possible. No dog photos and no tap dances. Just simple answers. And other than that, all they do is bear witness, until it is time to leave. At no point in the forest do any of the ghostly four give Harry hope. They give him his presence, until he drops the stone. And then they go.

Anne is never going to "get better" and Harry is going to have to confront Voldemort and die at his hand. But Harry would not have been able to do what he needed to do with his head held high if it wasn't for these four benevolent, calm presences at his side. The text tells us that "their presence was his courage." Harry would sacrifice himself without their company, but he does it more painlessly because he has it.

And that is what I need to learn from. Lily Potter does not show up to try to steer a change in the situation, or for any other tangible reason. She shows up because her presence is Harry's courage. And she knows that.

The problem with Anne's hopeless situation is partly, of course, the situation. It is beyond frustrating that a freak accident could cause so much pain and that with all the medical advances in the world we haven't been able to figure out a way to fix it. What I can do is believe that my presence matters and then show up when she asks me to, and leave when she tells me to—when she drops her stone. I can answer her direct questions, stand with her, and keep her company as she sits. I can be willing to sit with her quietly; she does not need my incessant, idle chatter.

There are rooms in which my advice will be required. There are rooms that are King's Cross station, in which I need to nudge and cajole, point or remind, take action and insist. But Anne's hospital room, as it turns out, is not one of them, at least not for me. There are other Dumbledores in Anne's hospital rooms. I need to look around in life, figure out if I am in the forest or at King's Cross, and if I find myself in the forest, believe that my presence is a blessing and sit down and shut up.

Or, at the very minimum, I have to behave as if I believe that my presence is a blessing and show up.

CHAPTER FOURTEEN

On Obsession in *The Great Gatsby*

Then he kissed her . . . and the incarnation was complete.

—Chapter 6, *The Great Gatsby*

When Stephanie and I started reading *Jane Eyre* as sacred, one the first things she did was hand me a letter called "The Ladder of Monks" by Guigo II, a Carthusian monk from Italy who died in 1193.

I love this letter. Its thesis is that reading can lead you to God. I do not believe in God, but this claim still feels deeply true to me. There have been moments of reading, most notably in my childhood, when I have felt understood by a person who is in absentia, represented only in fiction, conjured entirely in a stranger's imagination sometimes hundreds of years ago and hundreds or thousands of miles away. No one understood me at nine years old as Caddie Woodlawn did, and feeling her understanding of my inner life has to be like feeling the understanding of God. The fact that Carol Ryrie Brink could imagine feelings that I felt and had never been able to put words to and ascribe them to Caddie meant that I wasn't alone. And that has to be close to feeling God's understanding. It is being understood not for what you are willing to share with another but for what you would never tell another soul.

Guigo's idea of reading as a way to access God was particularly well articulated in his letter, but he is not alone in coming to this conclusion. Anne Frank seemed to believe that writing was a form of prayer as she sat in her attic. Nora Ephron said that "reading is escape; and the opposite of escape." People who love words often use them to rhapsodize about their love of words, and Guigo, in that way, is no different.

Guigo's letter says that one day he was working with his hands and body and "all at once four stages in spiritual exercise came into [his] mind: reading, meditation, prayer and contemplation." These are four distinct stages that Guigo spends much time outlining. I use words like *meditation*, *prayer*, and *contemplation* almost synonymously, diligently listing each of them when I am trying to talk vaguely about spiritual stuff, hoping for the words to work their magic on one another and conjure a fifth, unutterable word full of its own precise meaning that I have yet to find. Guigo separates these words as stages and gives each of the practices sharp edges of possibility.

Guigo makes no apologies for the fact that the outline he is making is for an audience of monks. For him, "these [four practices] make a ladder for monks by which they are lifted up from earth to heaven." This is not a path for a common man or woman. However, for a monk, Guigo delivers awesome news: Heaven is accessible on earth. You don't have to die to get there. Well, wait. A few sentences later the ladder does not take you to heaven, it just "touches heavenly secrets." Okay. Still pretty good. But again, this ability to touch heavenly secrets is not for a layperson. Being a monk seems to be a prerequisite if you want to touch heavenly secrets.

I think many of us have brief glimpses of heavenly secrets, and they are even told to us, appropriately enough, in literature.

Jay Gatsby, in F. Scott Fitzgerald's *The Great Gatsby*, has one of these miraculous moments, or at least the promise of one, and he is definitely not a monk. Gatsby is an early twentieth-century idea of an iconic American, willing to bootleg, lie, and bribe in order to accumulate as much wealth as possible in pursuit of a woman. However, he was not always that way. When he first met Daisy Fay, five years earlier, Gatsby was a young man in uniform, about to be sent overseas into World War I. He was charmed by the young, beautiful, and rich Daisy, and one night they found themselves on a walk alone. Jay Gatsby was a mere layperson who, while on this walk, for a short moment had access to one of these figurative ladders that Guigo describes.

Fitzgerald writes that "out of the corner of his eye Gatsby saw that the blocks of the sidewalks really formed a ladder and mounted to a secret place above the trees—he could climb to it, if he climbed alone, and once there he could suck on the pap of life, gulp down the incomparable milk of wonder." Gatsby sees that the sidewalk forms a ladder:

> He knew that when he kissed this girl, and forever wed his unutterable visions to her perishable breath, his mind would never romp again like the mind of God. So he waited, listening for a moment longer to the tuning-fork that had been struck upon a star. Then he kissed her . . . and the incarnation was complete.

According to Guigo, there are commonly four obstacles to being able to access God through his outlined practices:

> Unavoidable necessity, the good works of the active life, human frailty, worldly follies. The first can be excused, the second endured, the third invites

compassion, the fourth blame. Blame truly, for it would be better for the man who for love of the world turns his back on the goal, if he had never known God's grace, rather than, having known it, to retrace his steps.

Gatsby spends his life retracing his steps and trying to get back to that ladder, because the incarnation is complete for him, and the moment in which he could hear the pitch of the universe that he could have tuned himself against is now entirely bound up in Daisy. So he spends his life trying to get her back. And when he does actually manage to get Daisy back, it is not good enough; the ladder does not reappear out of the corner of his eye, and access to the incomparable milk of wonder is not reoffered, so his renewed relationship with Daisy implodes around him.

Guigo is attempting to offer a prescription so that monks do not spend their lives chasing that heavenly-secrets high like Gatsby does, only to be disappointed. Guigo has bottled that Caddie Woodlawn moment of my childhood and pushed it up three levels.

I think that I have more in common with Jay Gatsby than I do with Guigo II. When I read, my phone rings, or there is a knock on my door, or my dog reminds me it is time to take her on a walk, or I fall asleep. When I have moments in which I hear that "tuning-fork that has been struck upon a star," I do not try to tune my soul to it. I listen to its transcendent beauty for a brief moment, reveling in its generosity, knowing I am in a passing moment and that I cannot tune myself to it or change my life because of it. I have made too many promises, have too many obligations. The fact that I will not even consider tuning myself to this fork feels gendered to me. I was raised with my life backward-mapped from becoming a mom and to always be a dutiful daughter, so I have chosen to weigh myself down to earth so that I do not float away, rather than training myself to climb ladders or even look for them.

Is inebriating the thirsting soul with the dew of heavenly sweetness or gulping down the incomparable milk of wonder reserved for those who can afford to dedicate their lives to it? Will my incarnation of heavenly secrets be complete with a child I have, and will I therefore put too much effort into raising her, as I will be chasing purpose and meaning through her footsteps? Gatsby's moment is interrupted by kissing Daisy, but also by the war, which is impending at the moment they rush to kiss. It is love that turns him away from this opportunity to "touch heavenly secrets," but it is violence too.

There have been a lot of literary answers (which are my favorite types of answers) to this question of how and where to make a meaningful life. Virginia Woolf famously suggests murdering the angel of the house and finding a room of one's own. And part of me believes that I can follow Guigo's path through a certain kind of commitment. Maybe in a self-helpy reading-eight-minutes-a-day routine. As for me, these moments seem elusive and random, and the idea of putting myself in situations in which they could be more readily achieved always seems either suffocating or like a betrayal of myself and the people I love, whom I have made promises to that I take very seriously.

Imagining Gatsby and Guigo in conversation with each other gets us back to one of the essential questions that I carry around with me: What role will reading or seeking God have in our lives? What will we do when we hear that "elusive rhythm" beckoning us? And what will we do with the moments of disappointment when we try so hard and actively look and fight for those rhythms, "but they [make] no sound, and what [we] almost remembered [is] uncommunicable forever"? Do we go to monasteries, stay in one ivory tower or another in an attempt to work our way toward that shining vision? Do we count on our ability to work hard and access them between Instagram likes? Do we jump on the ladder when we see it out of the corner of our eye, or do we shackle ourselves to the ground so that we don't become addicted to the high?

Reading *Caddie Woodlawn* has saved me.

Our obsessions can free us. Reading *Caddie Woodlawn* has saved me. It has kept me company when I have felt painfully alone. But obsessions can also lead us to buying hundreds of expensive shirts—one in every color!—only to be left by the woman you protected when she accidentally killed someone. Obsessions are best when chosen, not when they come to us out of the corner of our eye.

Visions are best seen, acknowledged, and thanked, but not treated as the basis for shifting your whole life around.

Tool Kit on Sacred Readings:
Try This at Home

This is a "Kids, try this at home" chapter. Knowing that faith, rigor, and community are very broad ideas, I've written this chapter as a more granular, specific tool kit for ways in which you can go about treating a text as sacred. This tool kit works only for reading or dialogue in film and television. But I am sure that someone more creative than I can easily adapt it for non-word-based concepts like baseball.

First thing is picking your text. The truth is that just about anything you love works. You should go into this type of relationship with love already being at the center of your feelings toward the text. Treating a text as sacred is a long relationship.

You should only commit to something that you have a natural fondness for.

The thing to keep in mind is that in order for a text to be sacred, it has to be able to generate. It should generate ideas, thoughts, fan fiction, art, names for your children, and more. It has to be complicated enough that two people can read the same sentence and see different things in it. If something is too simple and has only one potential meaning, it is profane, not sacred. But while all of these measures of complexity are important, if you already love something, it is almost definitely generative and complicated. We do not tend to love the profane. Hate, in all its simplicity, is profane.

Once you have picked the text that you want to treat as sacred, there are a lot of tools for you to use to engage with it. If you can find a buddy who wants to commit to the same text and meet with you regularly to talk about it, all the better. But really, all you need to start is two things: (1) the faith that the more time you spend with the text, the more gifts it will give you, and (2) a commitment to engage with the text regularly (whatever that means for you). A community will help solidify the relationship but if you feel like you do not have a community to turn to, do not let that stop you from beginning.

There is a long history of scholars, readers, spiritual leaders, and Bible/Mishnah groups using the tools that I am about to outline here. There are also beautiful practices in religions other than Judaism and Christianity. Those practices are ones that I invite teaching on but never feel comfortable teaching myself. I modify the spiritual practices that I use for my atheist heart, and I feel comfortable doing so for my own religion of Judaism and for the culturally dominant religion in the United States, Christianity. But I do not feel comfortable doing that for Islam, Hinduism, Buddhism, Baha'i, and the countless other religions that have beautiful reading practices. If you are interested in seeking out those practices, I encourage you wholeheartedly.

Collecting Florilegia

As I mentioned, what I did with *Jane Eyre* was underline my favorite sentences, those that I believed could work in prayer. Now, I didn't know this at the time, but it turns out that even that practice has a religious root in it, although many of us collect quote journals without knowing or being impacted by the religious history of the practice. The practice of which I speak is collecting florilegia, which means "a gathering of flowers" in Latin.

I was taught this practice by Stephanie Paulsell, who told me about her father, a minister who reads his way through the book of Psalms. He reads a certain number of psalms each day and writes down the sentences that stick out to him, which are called sparklets. He writes them down in a journal, without annotating which psalms they are from, and then, when he's worked his way through the psalms, he reads his collection of sparklets—his florilegia—and reads it as if it is his own text. This then serves as a reflection tool: What stood out to him this time? What are these quotes saying to him about himself? What do the quotes mean next to one another, instead of in their usual places?

You treat this text that you have created as if it were its own sacred text, and then you go back and read the book again, and do it again. This can easily be done with any text, not just the psalms.

There are many ways to engage with your florilegia. For example, when you are reading as a group. I now lead pilgrimages with secular texts, and at the end of each day we all share our sparklet from that day. This can be a quote from the text that we have been reading or something that a fellow pilgrim has said. In this way, we learn to treat each other's words as sacred. I type up the sparklets that people share and then we spend a few minutes treating that new text as if it was sacred, simply remarking on what we notice about it. This can be done at the end of any book club meeting or at the end of reading any book in a book club; including your book club of one.

PaRDeS

Moses de León, a rabbi in the thirteenth century, is said to have been the first scholar to codify the idea of PaRDeS, but the idea itself dates back to the second century, to a famous story of four rabbis. PaRDeS is an acronym that stands for *p'shat* (which means surface), *remez* (hints), *d'rash* (seek), and *sud* (secret). But the word also means "orchard." The second-century idea is that PaRDeS is a location, an orchard of esoteric Torah knowledge.

Three of the four rabbis died or went mad; only the famous Rabbi Akiva made it out alive and well after being confronted with the spiritual realities of this orchard. The sacred reading practice of PaRDeS treats the text as an orchard. We cannot look at the entire orchard at once; we would go mad if we tried. But what we can do is pluck a single piece of fruit (or a sentence) and bite into it and see what it has to give us.

So, pick a sentence from your sacred text, either a sentence you love or a sentence at random; both practices are fun and worthwhile and give different rewards. The following is how Casper ter Kuile, my cohost on the *Harry Potter and the Sacred Text* podcast, and I use PaRDeS on a secular book (the Harry Potter series) that we treat as a sacred text.

1. *Step one, P (p'shat/surface)*: Ask yourself, "What is the intended meaning of the sentence? What did the author want me to get from it?"

2. *Step two, R (remez/hints)*: Pick one word from the sentence and then trace it throughout the seven Harry Potter books. If you were a rabbi, you'd pick a word and then think about all the different ways that word is in the

Bible. Then put the examples in conversation with one another. So, for example, if you picked the word *ark*, think about Noah's ark and the Ark of the Covenant. These are two very different uses of the same word in different books of the Bible (Noah's ark is in Genesis and the Ark of the Covenant is in Exodus). But you can derive meaning from the two uses of the word next to each other. If you think of the Ark of the Covenant as a ship that can get you through storms, then you see the Ten Commandments totally differently. You can now think of the Ten Commandments not as rules that restrict you, but as something that can guide you and keep you safe during horrible storms.

Or, for an example from the Harry Potter books, consider this sentence:

> *While Uncle Vernon, Aunt Petunia, and Dudley had gone out into the front garden to admire Uncle Vernon's new company car (in very loud voices, so that the rest of the street would notice it too), Harry had crept downstairs, picked the lock on the cupboard under the stairs, grabbed some of his books, and hidden them in his bedroom.*

You could pick a word like *car*. Then you could think through (or control-F through) the books and find that

Vernon takes pride in his cars, but so does Mr. Weasley. You could think about the Ford Anglia that means freedom for Harry in *Chamber of Secrets*, only to get Harry and Ron into a lot of trouble a few chapters later. You could think of the cars that take the Weasleys and Harry and Hermione to platform nine and three-quarters that the ministry lends them when it needs Harry, and that it does not lend them when Harry is a pain in its side. And so you could come to the conclusion that cars are power symbols in the world of the Harry Potter books; they are power grabs (like Vernon's) or power signaling (like the ministry's) or power being stolen (like Harry jumping into the Ford Anglia to his own freedom).

3. *Step three, D (d'rash/seek):* Ask yourself, "If this were my piece of scripture for the week and I were preaching on this sentence, what would I preach?" Or you could ask, "What is the lesson that I want to pull from this sentence?"

The trick with step three is that the lesson should not come just from the text. It should also come from all the hard work you did during step two. So maybe, if I were using the word *car*, I would write a lesson about power, that power earned (like the Ford Anglia showing up for Harry because he earned friendship and loyalty from Ron and Fred and George) is better than power grabbed (like Vernon's). These are often lessons that it turns out we need to hear ourselves.

4. *Step four, S (sud/secret)*: I love this step of PaRDeS because it is by far the most mystical practice that I engage in on a regular basis. The idea of *sud* is that you have done all this work—you have traced a word and written your lesson, and so now the text will open up one of its secrets to you. The way to do this on your own is simply to read the sentence one more time and then sit in silence with it. Hum it, recite it, or forget it. But see if a secret emerges. It might not, but it probably will more often than not. The secrets in and of themselves are beautiful gifts. But so is the reliability of an unknown reward for rigorous reading.

Lectio Divina

Lectio Divina (divine reading) is the Christian version of PaRDeS, but the differences are interesting and important. It is also a medieval practice and, like PaRDeS, has complicated roots, with one man getting credit for writing the idea down and codifying it a bit more than others. The Carthusian monk Guigo II said that reading could lead to prayer. He talked about reading as being similar to putting a grape in your mouth. There is the feel of the grape, the burst of the juice, the chewing, and then the nourishment. Following his four steps is like popping a piece of text in your mouth, extracting the juices, and then letting it nourish you.

Again, we have amended the traditional method of Lectio Divina for our own, secular devices. But the way I recommend using the four-step reading practice is as follows: As with PaRDeS, pick a sentence, either because it speaks to you or because you've selected it randomly.

Ask yourself what is literally going on in the sentence. For this you can read around the sentence for context; you want to remember where the scene is, what is going on, who is talking, and what this one moment that you have selected comes before and after.

Ask yourself what other stories this sentence reminds you of. This is a step for allegory. Does it remind you of a scene in Shakespeare? In what way? Does it remind you of a Greek myth? How does it differ? Does the sentence remind you of your favorite pop song? Why? List as many stories that this sentence reminds you of; it will expand your understanding of the text in front of you in magical ways.

Ask yourself what this reminds you of in your own life. Now that you have thought through stories in the world that this one sentence reminds you of, turn inward. Is there a moment from your own past that this reminds you of? This step is an invitation to see yourself in the text and to see yourself as less alone. You could easily be a character in this book and you are kindred with these characters in certain ways.

Ask yourself what action you feel called to because of the sentence and the practice that you have just done. It is best with this step to do something truly actionable. You don't want to say something vague like "Be more loving." You want to say, "I will call my sister in the next week." Invite the text to change your actions in the short run in order to give them a chance to change you in the long run.

Havruta

This is another Jewish practice, and it needs to be done in pairs, but that is in and of itself one of its gifts. It is delightful to treat a text as sacred with someone else. They will push you and keep you on track in your practice, and they will give you ideas that you never could have come up with on your own.

Havruta is an act of pair study that is rooted in the yeshiva tradition, in which a teacher mostly walks around the room while students sit in pairs day after day, with nothing but the Talmud between them. Their gathered heads and a book and a teacher nearby are all that they need for years of self-directed study.

The way we practice *havruta* on the podcast is that one of us brings a question about the text to the other. But the person who brings the question also has to bring an answer. This is a wonderful practice because it admits that all answers to questions are only partial answers. Any question worth asking is going to have many answers, and the truth is their composite; the truth is only captured in conversation.

In the next step of *havruta*, the other member of the pair, person B, listens to the question and answer, then gives their own response. Person B then asks a question inspired by the first one and provides an answer to begin the conversation. This can go on for as long as you like. Part of what I love about this practice is that it admits that we are all students and all teachers. It also allows for big swings and misses; you are trying answers on to see if they fit and doing so aloud with a partner.

Sacred Imagination

The last traditional sacred reading practice that I will write about here is called Ignatian imagination, but I have wrested it from poor Saint Ignatius and so now call it sacred imagination. It is named for Saint Ignatius of Loyola, a sixteenth-century monk and the founder of the Jesuit order, among many other things. Saint Ignatius (long before he was a saint) was a wealthy young Spanish man who loved Arthurian legends. He loved stories of chivalry and knights, which led him to joining the army at the age of seventeen. There are stories of him prancing around, loving the glamour of war. But then he got hit by a cannonball.

While he was convalescing at a Catholic hospital there were no stories of knights to read; there were only the Gospels. He found himself doing the same thing with the apostles and Jesus that he had done with the Knights of the Round Table: imagining himself into the story. He'd imagine himself fishing with Jesus, the air on his face, the tackle on his fingers, the smell of the fish as they sat in the boat.

This kind of imagination can change the way you see a scene. Pick a scene from your text and imagine on behalf of each of your senses: What is this character seeing, smelling, touching, tasting, hearing? I was not a big believer in this practice until I read *Harry Potter and the Sorcerer's Stone* and read about the troll attack from Hermione's perspective. It had never occurred to me how truly terrified Hermione must have been until I imagined the cold of the bathroom tiles on my back, the horrible smell of the troll, the water spraying, and the sheer noise of it all. I then realized that Hermione does not just become friends with the boys because they've been through something difficult together; she has realized that she would have died if they hadn't come. She realizes that you need friends to survive.

Acknowledgments

Ellen and Anna Mueller, thank you for letting me into your family and for being two of the loves of my life. You are my favorite monsters. And to Peter, thank you for sending me down to write even when I pouted, and for celebrating with me every time I got another thousand words down. Your love is the stuff of Romance novels and I love you.

My brothers, David and Jonathan Zoltan, whose love, lives, and support are impossible to separate from who I am. And my sister-in-law, Suzanne, one of the funniest writers I know, who is a beacon of generosity and happens to have birthed my gorgeous niece and nephew to boot.

Kim Eisenstein, who is a person in her own right, but is also my superpower and probably the person I admire most in the world. Julia Grace Argy, for always walking with me and usually leading the way. Ariana Nicole Nedelman for being my imagined audience and the person I write to impress. Casper ter Kuile for making me laugh, making me feel strong, and making my career. Jen Chau for pushing me even when I really didn't want it and for letting me rest when I really, really didn't want it. Dana Greer for making me laugh and telling me that I'm perfect for the past fifteen years. Nick Bohl for mocking my baggage but then carrying it.

Olivia Hamilton, Abby Engelstad, and Lauren Taylor, for being in my "thesis support group," for surviving the Old Testament with me, for being part of what made div school great, and for reminding me what it is to be a good person. And then, of course, to Mike Motia, facilitator of said support group, who literally believed in this project before I did. The *Jane Eyre* class members of that group at the Hub all those years ago, especially Ingrid Norton.

Rosy Hosking, who read my first Bertha essay, and Robert, Carla, and Marian Majovski, my god-family.

Chloe Angyal, my low-key soul mate.

Brigid Goggin, whom I would bike twenty miles in the dark for again and again.

Molly Vaughan, for twenty years of generosity and true love.

Rachel Williams, for book, puppy, and baby talk like nowhere else.

Dana Kuhn, who was literally with me when I started this book.

Emmy Wohlgemuth, my fellow adventurer.

Ndidiamaka Oteh, who is as beautiful as the bouquets of flowers she spends too long putting together.

Michelle Cherney, my favorite aunt.

Rebecca Ledley, my first family member in HDS land.

Graham and Vickie Cole, whose marriage called me to chaplaincy.

Nick Barber, my favorite justice ninja.

Brooke Breit (and Frankie and Sadie), whom I have been embarrassing and loving for twenty years.

Amanda Morejon, my sister.

Robby Boyer, my extra brother.

Duke Rodda, whom I hated until I loved.

Bryce Gilfillian, who was my first fan but not before I was his fan.

Amy Zeide, for giving me a home on a night when I had nowhere to go.

The beautiful Grey family (especially my Isa).

Acknowledgments

Francesca Childs, for being a coparent and always having my back.

Lauren Taylor for years of musicals, sparkling wine, and endless conversation and support.

Colette Potts, for showing up that day, and again and again.

Elizabeth Slade, the best listener I know and an absolute gift, and Bob Filbin, for giving me Harry Potter and, more importantly, Rory.

The whole Potts family, for always being happy to have me as long as I bring cake.

Aaron Fogelson, Nina Srivastava, Eana Meng, Julie Baldassano, Zohra Yaqhubi, Suzanne Garrison, Judith Giller-Leinwohl, John and Esther Freidman, Nitzan Pelman, and all my friends who have come to live shows, gone on writing retreats with me, designed pilgrimages with me (Liz), given legal advice, listened to pilots of podcasts, discussed books with me, and been the best friends a person could ask for. I also have made many of you work with me over the years because I just can't get enough of your brains and hearts. I'm sorry to just list you all. You deserve more, but this is all I got.

The team at Not Sorry Productions: Maggie Needham, Meghan Kelly, Amanda Madigan, Hannah Goldbach, Ariana Martinez, Norah Murphy, Lauren Taylor (again again, never enough), and the incredible *Harry Potter and the Sacred Text* and *Hot and Bothered* communities. Thank you for making dreams that I did not think to have come true. Thank you for forgiving my mistakes and hearing me with generosity when I stumble onto something true. With special gratitude to those of you who joined me on our *Jane Eyre* pilgrimage; so many of the ideas in this book came from our conversations, and I hope one day we can have tea and cake in Haworth again.

My teachers: Amy Hollywood, Terry Tempest Williams, Andrew Lamas, Dan Smith, Nan Goodman, Cheryl Giles, Kevin Madigan, and Dara Horn. And to those amazing high school teachers: Ms. Wong, Madam O'Hanlon, Mr. Koransky, and Mrs. Creasy, who taught me how to write. You all deserve statues. Especially to Matt Potts, who, among other things, came up with the format of this book, would answer every annoying text I sent, whom I have sadly become completely dependent on in my writing, and who was this book's first reader. Also to all my students over nine years of being with you; you were wonderful teachers.

My agent, Lisa DiMona. I don't deserve you, but I'll keep you. Nora Long, you poor, brilliant woman who read my proposal eighteen times and made it the best version you could wring out of me, and Lauren Carsley for seamlessly picking up where Nora left off. My editor, Marian Lizzi, thank you for saving me from myself and making me sound smart and being such an empathetic reader. And thank you to everyone at Penguin Random House who made this book possible: Carla Iannone, Alyssa Adler, Rachel Dugan, Farin Schlussel, Casey Maloney, and Rachel Ayotte.

And, of course, to my grandparents: Deszo Zoltan, Elizabeth Zoltan, Ruth Steif Rogier, and Abraham Alain Rosenberg Rogier. I'm sorry for any mistakes I make in representing your stories and thank you for so much, but especially for surviving.

I already dedicated the book to them, but at last: Stephanie, there are no words, so I tried to give you seventy thousand. Dad, thank you for being so worried about my life and career that you wrote me a memo and then loved and supported me once I rejected that memo. And Mom, my greatest wish is to be like you.

Sources

Arendt, Hannah. *Eichmann in Jerusalem: A Report on the Banality of Evil*. New York: Penguin Books, 2006.

Armstrong, Karen. *The Lost Art of Scripture: Rescuing the Sacred Texts*. London: Bodley Head, 2019.

Awkward, Michael. *Soul Covers: Rhythm and Blues Remakes and the Struggle for Artistic Identity (Aretha Franklin, Al Green, Phoebe Snow)*. Durham, NC: Duke University Press, 2007.

Barker, Juliet R. V. *The Brontës: Wild Genius on the Moors; The Story of a Literary Family*. New York: Pegasus Books, 2012.

Bloomfield, Morton W. "*The Divine Comedy. Vol. I: Inferno*. Dante Alighieri and Charles S. Singleton. *Dante's Inferno*. Dante Alighieri, Mark Musa." *Speculum* 48, no. 1 (Jan. 1973): 127–29. doi: 10.2307/2856280.

de Botton, Alain. *How Proust Can Change Your Life*. New York: Vintage International, 1998.

Dew, Spencer. Review of *Citizen: An American Lyric* by Claudia Rankine. *Religious Studies Review* 41, no. 4 (2015): 184–85. doi: 10.1111/rsr.12255_3.

Gaskell, Elizabeth Cleghorn, and Elisabeth Jay. *The Life of Charlotte Brontë*. New York: Penguin Books, 1997.

Gay, Roxane. *Bad Feminist: Essays*. New York: Harper Perennial, 2014.

Gilbert, Sandra M., and Susan Gubar. *The Madwoman in the Attic: The Woman Writer and the Nineteenth-Century Literary Imagination*. 2nd ed. New Haven, CT: Yale University Press, 2000.

Guigo et al. *The Ladder of Monks: A Letter on the Contemplative Life and Twelve Meditations*. Collegeville, MN: Cistercian Publications, 1981.

Gyasi, Yaa. *Homegoing*. New York: Alfred A. Knopf, 2016.

Hillesum, Etty, and Eva Hoffman. *Etty Hillesum: An Interrupted Life: The Diaries, 1941–1943; and Letters from Westerbork*. New York: Henry Holt, 1996.

Kugel, James L. *How to Read the Bible: A Guide to Scripture, Then and Now.* New York: Free Press, 2007.

Kuile, Casper ter. *The Power of Ritual: Turning Everyday Activities into Soulful Practices.* New York: HarperOne, 2020.

Lewis, John. *Across That Bridge: Life Lessons and a Vision for Change.* New York: Hyperion, 2012.

MacIntyre, Alasdair C. *Edith Stein: A Philosophical Prologue, 1913–1922.* Lanham, MD: Rowman & Littlefield, 2006.

McCarthy, Michael. "*In the Dream House: A Memoir* by Carmen Maria Machado (Review)." *Prairie Schooner* 94, no. 2 (2020): 193–94. doi: 10.1353/psg.2020.0069.

Monk, Nicholas. Review of *Cormac McCarthy and the Signs of Sacrament* by Matthew L. Potts. *Journal of American Studies* 51, no. 1 (2017): E10. doi: 10.1017/S0021875816001675.

Nhat Hanh, Thich. *Peace Is Every Breath: A Practice for Our Busy Lives.* New York: HarperOne, 2011.

O'Donohue, John. *To Bless the Space Between Us: A Book of Blessings.* New York: Doubleday, 2008.

Ortberg, Mallory. *Texts from Jane Eyre: And Other Conversations with Your Favorite Literary Characters.* New York: Henry Holt, 2014.

Paulsell, Stephanie. *Religion Around Virginia Woolf.* University Park, PA: Penn State University Press, 2019.

Rhys, Jean. *Wide Sargasso Sea.* New York: Penguin Books, 1990.

Saunders, George. *Congratulations, by the Way: Some Thoughts on Kindness.* New York: Random House, 2014.

Simpson, Jessica. *Open Book.* New York: Dey Street Books, 2020.

Smart, Elizabeth, and Chris Stewart. *My Story.* New York: St. Martin's Griffin, 2014.

Snyder, Timothy. *On Tyranny: Twenty Lessons from the Twentieth Century.* New York: Tim Duggan Books, 2017.

Teresa of Ávila and Mirabai Starr. *The Interior Castle.* Newberry, FL: Bridge-Logos, 2008.

van der Kolk, Bessel A. *The Body Keeps the Score: Brain, Mind, and Body in the Healing of Trauma.* New York: Viking, 2014.

Weil, Simone. *Waiting for God.* New York: Harper Perennial Modern Classics, 2009.

Williams, Terry Tempest. *Erosion: Essays of Undoing.* New York: Sarah Crichton Books/Farrar, Straus and Giroux, 2019.

Wood, James. *How Fiction Works.* New York: Vintage, 2009.

Woolf, Virginia, and Jeanne Schulkind. *Moments of Being.* 2nd ed. San Diego: Harcourt Brace Jovanovich, 1985.